New Shoes

It's been a long journey to get this book from page to print! With special thanks to all the brave women and men who have taken part in the Into The Light programmes – you have been my inspiration. I so appreciate the support of: Ruth, Sadie, Nicky, Janet, Sophie, Hazel, Jo, Jilly, Terri, Yinka – and of course Barbara: everything changed when I met you. Biggest thanks go to my amazing husband Jonny and daughter Dee Dee.

New Shoes

*Stepping out of the shadow
of sexual abuse and
living your dreams*

REBECCA MITCHELL

LION

A Lion Book
an imprint of
Lion Hudson plc
Wilkinson House, Jordan Hill Road,
Oxford OX2 8DR, England
www.lionhudson.com
ISBN 978 0 7459 5552 0

Distributed by:
UK: Marston Book Services, PO Box 269, Abingdon, Oxon, OX14 4YN
USA: Trafalgar Square Publishing, 814 N. Franklin Street, Chicago, IL 60610
USA Christian Market: Kregel Publications, PO Box 2607, Grand Rapids,
Michigan 49501

First edition 2011
10 9 8 7 6 5 4 3 2 1 0

Acknowledgments
The stories in this book are based on the lives of real people. However,
either permission has been obtained for inclusion, or they have been
disguised so that it is not possible to identify them.

Main cover image © Harry Choi/TongRo Image Stock/Corbis; author
portrait © Zelda Meyburgh (www.zeldameyburgh.co.uk)

A catalogue record for this book is available
from the British Library

Typeset in 10/13 New Baskerville ITC by BT
Printed in Great Britain by Clays Ltd, St Ives plc

CONTENTS

INTRODUCTION

IT'S NOT YOU, IT'S ME

"I think I'm done." My boyfriend sounded exhausted but firm. I knew the end was coming as it had before, but this time I was genuinely distressed. "Maybe we can try again..." I faltered. "I've had enough," he snapped. "I don't know whether I'm coming or going with you... you're all over the place. You want me... you don't want me. You can't make a decision, so I'm going to." Salty tears began falling down my face. Why did my relationships always end this way? Why did I always pick boyfriends who could never understand me properly? Why did I love and hate them at the same time? Was it them or was it me?

On the other side of the same town Josie is half way through a bottle of vodka. Her relationship has also ended. Her partner has left her because he feels her drinking has got out of hand. Through her alcoholic haze she is contemplating why she has to spend so much of her time trying to block out her past with spirits. Her thoughts turn to her stepfather – she doesn't know why she hates him so much. Her brother certainly doesn't; his life was transformed with the new money that came into the house when their new "dad" arrived. Without warning her mind runs over an ugly night when she was twelve involving him and an incident in the bathroom. She shudders and tries to force the images from her mind. She had wanted to tell her mum, but her silence was ensured by his threats that speaking out would "break up the new family" – and anyway, she doubted her mother would believe her.

Josie is drinking because she is trying to forget the huge trauma she has experienced. I am running from relationships because I find the feelings of intimacy too frightening.

Josie and I have both been sexually abused by people close to us – we have been severely betrayed by our families and communities, and the effects on our lives have been catastrophic. I'm blaming my boyfriend. But the truth is, the problem is with me and the damage I have been caused in my past.

You are not alone

If you have picked up this book the chances are that you (or someone you know) have experienced the trauma of rape or sexual abuse. Perhaps your life story is different from mine or Josie's, but I imagine you can relate to our shame and pain. Perhaps you have never faced this before, or maybe this is another in a long line of books you have reached for in the hope of finding an answer. Maybe just handling this book is making you feel very self-conscious.

Obviously I don't know where you are right now. But one thing I do know is that you are not alone. Sexual abuse is one of the most prevalent destructive forces operating in societies all over the world, and yet one of the worst torments of the abuse is the desire (both of victim and perpetrator) to keep it in the dark.

Kept hidden, the inward agony of the past can only get worse, and this often means that outwardly destructive behaviour begins to take hold, drawing a life that is full of potential into loneliness and despair.

And yet, is there hope?

As a survivor myself, and as someone who has supported others for over seventeen years, I can say – personally and professionally – absolutely yes! It can be hard work. But at the same time it is hugely empowering to know that you can make the changes to your life that you want.

It is my desire that this book may play a small part in offering you some support on your journey. It is written from my own experience of living through many years of sexual abuse as a child – and also as a professional who has run support groups and workshops for people who have experienced sexual abuse.

But why should we face the past? Is there any real point in looking backwards? It was a long time ago, so isn't it all in the past?

Why abuse gets in the way of your life

The problem with pain is that when you bury it, you bury it alive, and it stays there, hidden, but often very actively surfacing in your life in subconscious and strange ways. You may say that in some areas of your life you function very well; that you do not have any difficulties with relating to people at work, or that in your career you are very successful. However, the problems around abuse most frequently arise in relationships. Often when you enter into a relationship with someone, especially with a possible partner or close friend, the fear of abuse will surface.

This is because we can live well in performing mode, but not very well when we are in intimate relationships. It's like having two lives but only one body to live them in! In one area of your life you are doing well, but in another area you can be very damaged and not able to cope at all. This can leave you feeling lonely and isolated.

Mary is a successful business woman working in the highly competitive TV industry. She has moved further up the management ladder than many women and is not even thirty yet. However, Mary got home last night to find her housemate had packed her bags and left. This would not usually be a problem, but this was the sixth housemate who had left in two years; they couldn't cope with Mary's controlling behaviour.

Mary is outwardly very confident, but she too has suffered sexual abuse by a relative. This has left her with huge trust issues towards anyone she is close to. Mary is effective at work, but outside that arena she does not relate to others very well.

Mary, Josie, and my twenty-three-year-old self were all struggling with our relationships because the damage of the abuse we suffered in the past was so intense. Of course, those around us also have problems, but some of our main difficulties in life lie within us.

It is my hope in writing this book that you will be able to recognize some patterns of behaviour that may not be helpful to you. I also hope that you may be able to pick up some ideas of how these patterns could be changed so that you can develop closer connections with people you care about, and perhaps build a different kind of life for the future.

What you may feel reading this book
Be prepared! Reading this book and thinking about abuse may bring up some strong and seemingly overwhelming feelings.

Creating a safe space
It is a good idea to create a safe place in your room or house while you are reading this book. This will be a place you can go to if anxieties arise. Make an agreement with yourself that as long as you are in that spot, you'll be safe. Also make an agreement that if you start to feel out of control or afraid of what you might say or do, you will go to that place and stay there. You can also breathe one breath at a time, until the feeling passes. Your safe place could be a window seat, a bed, or a favourite reading chair.

Reaching out
List any friends that you could call if you were feeling anxious:

Name	*Phone number*

Is there anything else that would help you if you were feeling upset or scared – for example, putting on a favourite CD or reading a comforting book?

What to do if you feel you need support

If you are feeling overwhelmed by your situation and are finding it difficult to function, it would be a good idea to talk to your doctor. They may refer you to a counsellor. If it's the middle of the night and you need someone to talk to urgently, you can call the Samaritans on 0845 790 9090 or go to their website, www.samaritans.org. If you are feeling suicidal, do not try to cope alone. Always go to your doctor or contact the Samaritans.

Talking to close friends or a partner about our feelings is a good step too, but sometimes we need the objective help of a professional counsellor. Counselling and therapy are sometimes portrayed in the media as being highly expensive and only for celebrities who want to escape an ex-partner or the paparazzi! This is not the case. Counselling is quite widely available and falls within most people's budgets. In the UK you may be able to access free counselling on the NHS if you speak to your doctor.

If you have never had counselling for being sexually abused I would recommend that you seriously consider it. Having the support of someone who has experience and compassion is an invaluable tool in the healing process. I would even go as far as to ask you what is stopping you – and (to press my point!) is that a good enough reason?

Spending one hour a week in counselling for six months can be a turn-around factor and help you towards a happier life and better relationships.

Considering counselling

Once you have decided to get some help, the next question is where to go and what to look for in a counsellor or therapist. The choice offered on the internet or in a directory such as *Yellow Pages* or yell.com can be quite overwhelming.

Here are some tips on trying to find a counsellor:

Check they are part of a professional association for counsellors

You should check that your counsellor belongs to a professional body which has professional standards and accountability. The British Association for Counsellors and Psychotherapists (BACP) is the main body in the UK representing counselling at national and international levels. The BACP aims to promote counselling and raise standards of training and practice, and produces a directory in which there is a list of counsellors. In order to be on the BACP directory, counsellors need to have met certain standards of training and experience. They will all also be covered by a code of ethics and practice and a complaints procedure. However, there are other professional bodies that also require their members to have reached certain training levels and which are bound by a practice code. These include the United Kingdom Council for Psychotherapy (UKCP) and the British Psychological Society (BPS).

What kind of approach does the counsellor have?

There are many different kinds of approaches to counselling work. Some counsellors are specifically trained in one theory – for example, person-centred counselling. Or counsellors may be trained in one particular area of counselling – for instance, marriage counselling. As a general rule, which theory the counsellor follows may not be as important as the experience they have in the area in which you would like support. If you would like more details about different counselling theories there is some helpful information on the BACP site (www. bacp.co.uk) in the section on "Seeking a Therapist": go to "Explanation of Theoretical Approaches".

Does the counsellor have experience in the area you would like to talk about?

Some counsellors are specially trained or have a great deal of experience in a particular area of counselling. For example, a counsellor may be trained to work with couples or with an addiction. If you are seeking help for a specific issue, like sexual abuse, then ask the counsellor when you first speak to them if they have experience and training in this area. You could also ask them if they have been able to help other clients struggling with this issue to resolve some of their difficulties.

How long are counselling sessions?

Most counselling sessions last for what is known as "the fifty-minute hour". This means that the sessions are actually fifty minutes long, and then the counsellor may spend the final ten minutes making notes on that session and preparing for the next one. However, if you join group counselling, the session can be much longer – up to an hour and a half. If you are travelling a long way to your session and are seeing your counsellor less than once a week, some counsellors are willing to extend the time. You could ask about this on your first contact with the counsellor.

How much could you expect to pay?
Most counsellors charge for their services. However, there is often quite a wide variety of prices. Some counsellors operate what is known as a "sliding scale" for fees. This means you will be asked to disclose how much you earn and then the fees will be charged accordingly. For example, if you are a student you will be paying less than someone who is earning £30,000 per annum. Also, counsellors may charge more for counselling couples. Some counsellors do have free places, but this is the exception rather than the rule. However, some counselling services will offer reduced rate counselling. You can also ask your doctor if they have a counsellor working as part of their practice who offers free counselling.

That first call or email
It can be quite daunting to pick up the phone or send an email to a complete stranger to talk about things that are very personal to you. Try to remember they are there to help you. If you choose to make contact over the phone, you can call most counsellors in the daytime or evening. Often they will have an answerphone service as they may be working at the time you call. Don't be put off by this: leave a message and they will get back to you. When you first call or email here are some questions you could consider asking:

- What hours do they work?
- Do they work weekends or evenings?
- How often are sessions held? (Some counsellors see their clients weekly, others twice a month, some twice a week.)
- What is their theoretical approach? What experience do they have (how long have they been a counsellor)?
- How much experience do they have of counselling people who have been sexually abused?
- What are their fees? Do they charge for an initial session? (Some counsellors do not charge for this, others charge less for the first session.)

Practical questions to ask

When you contact the counsellor you have chosen, there are some practical questions to consider.

- Do they have a waiting area? (Some counsellors do not, which means you have to wait outside until your appointment.)
- Is there a toilet you can use?
- Are there local transport facilities? Is there a bus or train service nearby?
- Is there somewhere to park your car and do you have to pay for parking?

Is this counsellor right for you?

For some people it is important to have a counsellor who reflects their own lifestyle, choices, race, sexuality, values, or beliefs. For example, if you are a Muslim you may feel more comfortable with a Muslim counsellor who shares your faith. Or if you are a woman you may prefer to see a female counsellor. There is another side to this, however. If, for example, you are struggling with your relationships with men, it could be to your advantage to see a male counsellor, who could help you to work on the issues you are finding challenging. Some counsellors will openly advertise their religion or sexuality so that clients know this; others keep this information private. However, if there is something that is really important to you, ask your counsellor when you first meet them where they stand on this issue, so you are both clear about this in your minds.

Booking an initial session
When you attend your first session, try to arrive with some specific areas you want to work on. For example, instead of saying, "I feel unhappy", try to think about what it is specifically that you are unhappy about. Perhaps it could be, "I have recently broken up with a partner" or "I have been sexually abused as a child and I want to look at how it is affecting my life today." This will help you to know what you want to work on during your sessions.

During the first session it is usual for your counsellor to ask you about your past; although it may seem daunting or you might think them a bit nosy, they are actually trying to see how they can help you to get where you want to be. So expect to be asked some personal questions.

Drawing up a contract
During the first meeting your counsellor may ask you if you want to book a series of sessions with them. This means that together you will sign a contract that both of you agree on, stating the number of sessions, the fees and the time of the sessions. Both parties then agree to keep this contract, and if at the end of it you feel you need more sessions, you will sign a new contract together.

Specialist services

When you are looking for counsel and support you can try services that have been set up specifically for people who have been sexually abused; for example, a rape or sexual abuse support service. Counsellors there are both trained and experienced in dealing with this issue. You can do this through an internet search. These services often charge a low rate or may even be free. However, these services are often very oversubscribed so you may have to join a waiting list before being seen. There is a list of support services at the back of this book.

Keep going!

Lastly, don't give up! If the first counsellor you contact does not meet your requirements keep going until you find someone that can give you the support you need. Help is definitely out there.

At the moment the problem may be with us – but with the right information and support this can be changed. I hope this book will be a companion for you on your journey and, along with your counsellor or support group, will enable you to have deeper relationships and a more satisfying life.

Starting the journey

In this book we will tackle some of the consequences of being sexually abused and discuss some solutions to the problems or feelings they may raise. In the next ten chapters we will cover the following issues:

Shame

- What shame is and how it impacts us
- How we tend to carry the shame that belongs to the abuser, and ways to give it back

Memories
- Why we bury them
- How they can help us deal with our past

Anger
- Why anger from the past can control us today
- How we can use anger constructively

Families
- How they shape our ideas and the roles we play in relationships
- Why we may like to choose a different role

Relationships
- The damaging effects of powerlessness and betrayal
- Ideas for rebuilding trust

Sex
- How the pain of the past interrupts us now
- Ideas about how we can learn to relax

Forgiveness
- Why it is different from reconciliation
- Why we should forgive and why we shouldn't

First, however, it is important to understand just how many people are affected by child sexual abuse and the impact it has both on them and on our society.

Checkout sheet: Introduction

In my role as a group facilitator I always have a "checkout" at the end of each session. This is a short time which gives us a chance to reflect on the session and what it has meant to us before we leave. I have put checkout sheets at the end of each chapter to give you the opportunity to reflect on any thoughts or feelings it has raised for you.

1. How do you feel now you've finished the introduction? If you feel shaky, take some time out before you go on to the first chapter.

2. Do you feel free to express your anger and pain with others present or do you usually do your crying on your own?

3. How difficult would it be for you to share how you really feel with others?

4. Do you have any plans to confide in someone more freely; for example, a counsellor?

5. If not, what is stopping you?

6. Have you thought of somewhere that could be your "safe place"?

CHAPTER ONE

IS IT JUST ME?

One of the most isolating effects of sexual abuse is that you feel so alone. Factually, however, this is not the case. Several studies over the last thirty years have shown that child abuse is extremely prevalent in our society. It is estimated that one in four women and one in six men have been sexually abused as children.

How widespread is sexual abuse?

In 1991 a survey carried out by the Child Abuse Studies Unit of the University of North London revealed that one in two girls (59 per cent) and one in four boys (27 per cent) in the United Kingdom will experience sexual abuse by the time they are eighteen. The definition of abuse they used was any event or interaction which the young person reported as abusive or unwanted before the age of eighteen.[1]

Other surveys also confirm the high occurrence of sexual abuse in British society: A study undertaken in 1986 found that 38 per cent of girls are sexually abused before the age of eighteen.[2] Another study carried out in 1990 showed that 16 per cent of boys are sexually abused before the age of eighteen.[3]

A more recent study conducted in 2000 also suggests child sexual abuse continues to be very prevalent in the UK, with 11 per cent of boys under sixteen and 21 per cent of girls under sixteen experiencing sexual abuse during their childhood.[4]

In 2008 ChildLine reported a 50 per cent increase in calls relating to sexual abuse since 2005.[5]

The internet has made images of child sexual abuse more readily available. In October 2007, a report by the Internet Watch Foundation said that about 1.5 million adults in the UK had seen child abuse online. It also said that more than a third of all child sexual abuse sites contained images of the most severe kinds of abuse. Nearly one in three children appearing on the sites were under six years old, while one in twenty were under the age of two.

Sadly, this is not a problem that is confined to the West. The Bangkok-based international child protection campaign group ECPAT (End Child Prostitution, Child Pornography and Trafficking of Children for Sexual Purposes) has said that across the Middle East and South Asia, marriage contracts can be found which are being used as a cloak for child abuse.[6] Child rape is also used as a "weapon of war" in areas of conflict, such as the Congo in 2010. In October 2010 more than 1,000 teachers in Kenya were sacked for sexually abusing girls: most of the victims were aged between twelve and fifteen. There are also extremely sad stories from poor countries such as Afghanistan, where there are reports of girls as young as six being sold off in marriage for money by fathers who are in debt and feel they have no other financial choice.

These statistics can seem very cold and impersonal, yet all these figures represent individuals – people whose lives are severely damaged by abuse.

What is abuse?
Child sexual abuse occurs when a person involves a child in any activity which that person expects to lead to their own sexual arousal or gratification. This does not just mean intercourse. It can mean touching, groping, masturbation by the abuser, taking photographs, exposing themselves to the

NEW SHOES

child, talking in sexually explicit terms, internet abuse in chat rooms, peeping at the victim while in the bath or undressing. These all constitute sexual abuse.

However, it is important to understand that what is critical is not necessarily the technicalities of the abuse, but the effect on the person.

Abuse is defined as follows by the Department of Health, Education and Home Office in their 1999 document, "Working Together to Safeguard Children":

> Sexual abuse involves forcing or enticing a child or young person to take part in sexual activities, whether or not the child is aware of what is happening. The activities may involve physical contact, including penetrative (e.g. rape or buggery) or non-penetrative acts. They may include non-contact activities, such as involving children in looking at, or in the production of, pornographic material or watching sexual activities, or encouraging children to behave in sexually inappropriate ways.

It is often hard to accept that abuse that is not strictly physical can be so damaging – for instance, non-contact sexual abuse very often leaves the victim wondering whether anything happened at all. Rakesh is now in her thirties and cannot remember any sexual abuse that involved actual physical contact. Yet her life and relationships reflect the violations she suffered as a result of being voyeuristically stared at by her grandfather as a child. This deeply offended her and damaged her view of herself and her sexuality. It doesn't have to be physical touch to count as sexual abuse: if a child receives degrading sexual comments, even if they do not fully understand what is being said, these will still have a lasting effect and can cause turmoil within the child.

· ·

Who are abusers?

On TV and in the media abusers are usually portrayed as strangers in the park wearing dirty raincoats. Of course that does happen, but the reality is that most people are abused by people they know and are involved with.

Most people admit that abuse goes on, but no one wants to admit that it happens in their community and especially not in their family. It is simply too terrifying for people to think about. This could be why abusers are often demonized in the media and compared to monsters. People feel safer thinking about abusers this way as it makes them think they will be able to spot them – giving them power in the situation. Thinking that an abuser could be a normal person – someone they know and even like – makes people feel frightened and powerless.

Fay's family were hurt and angry when Fay told them she had been abused by her grandfather. Surely the kindly old man they had recently buried who had been so generous at Christmas and birthdays was not capable of a crime such as this? Fay was then ostracized for some years and was not invited to family events – until her cousin also came forward with a similar story. Fay had been brave enough to confront her past, and had to face the consequences of not being believed by the family who should have supported her.

However, research supports Fay's case as it shows that most abusers are known to the victim. They are not strangers at all. Ninety-six per cent of children who called ChildLine in 2008 because they were being sexually abused knew the abuser.[7]

Abusers appear no different from any other man or woman and come from every social stratum – builders, doctors, teachers, or clergymen. Indeed, in a survey of convicted offenders of internet child porn carried out by the NSPCC in April 2010, one in four held a "position of trust", including teachers, clergy, and medical professionals.[8]

· ·

Social scientist and author Dr Diana Russell[9] completed a study of 152 women who had been incestuously sexually abused in their childhood. She found that there was no abuser stereotype regarding education or socio-economic class:

- 32 per cent of the perpetrators had upper middle class occupations
- 34 per cent had middle class occupations
- 34 per cent had lower class occupations

There was also no extraordinary racial or ethnic predominance among the abusers beyond that of the general population.

Women as well as men sexually abuse boys and girls. The tragic case of Vanessa George's conviction in the UK in 2009 testifies to that, and yet this side of sexual abuse is often met by even more disbelief and horror. Research by the NSPCC in 2005 found that women are "responsible for up to 5 per cent of all sexual offences committed against children".[10]

The impact of ChildLine

It could be said that it is only relatively recently that professionals in the UK – for example, doctors and teachers – have been mobilized to become aware of child sexual abuse in their communities. The ball actually started rolling after a survey was taken in 1986 by the BBC TV programme *That's Life*, asking viewers for their help in an investigation into child abuse. Three thousand adults (of whom 90 per cent were women) completed the survey and 90 per cent of them said they had experienced child sexual abuse.

As a direct result of this, child care professionals and the voluntary sector established ChildLine, a confidential helpline for children. Today ChildLine continues to provide help and counsel for children and the statistics around sexual abuse continue to be high. In the twenty years between 1986 and 2006, ChildLine counselled more than 175,000 children about sexual abuse. ChildLine says, "Children often don't tell about abuse because they have been threatened into keeping silent or made to feel ashamed and guilty." Sadly the shame and silence often continues into adulthood.

There is some positive news, though: children are now calling earlier in the cycle of sexual abuse than they did when ChildLine first started. Nearly 65 per cent of children calling ChildLine in 1986 said the sexual abuse had been going on for more than a year; by 2006 that figure had dropped to 23 per cent.[11]

Legacy of abuse

It would be comforting to think that once a traumatic childhood is over, the adult will go on to live a much happier life. Sadly this is rarely the case: research shows us that the legacy of child abuse in adults can be very damaging.

The Princes Trust carried out a survey of violent offenders (that is, offenders kept under the Section 53 ruling) and found that three in ten of them had experienced child sexual abuse.[12] Most had experienced it at home and some went on to be re-abused in residential children's homes.

A survey carried out in 1997 by HM Inspectorate of Prisons discovered that 30 to 70 per cent of women prisoners have been sexually abused.[13] And research in the USA shows that those who have experienced serious childhood trauma such as physical, sexual or emotional abuse may have twice the rate of cancer, heart disease, and chronic bronchitis as those who have not experienced such trauma.[14]

Other research shows that abuse survivors are more likely to become suicidal. An American study showed that adults who experienced child sexual abuse are twelve times more likely to attempt suicide than those who did not.[15] Survivors of sexual abuse are additionally more likely to suffer from addiction and related problems. A United Kingdom study in a regional patient drug detoxification unit found that 90 per cent of women and 37 per cent of men had been victims of childhood sexual abuse.[16]

Perhaps this isn't surprising when you realize that research shows that many abused children do not tell anyone of their abuse until they are adults. Carrying the weight of such a painful secret is bound to have an effect on physical and emotional welfare.

Other repercussions for victims today may be less dramatic but are personally just as devastating, ranging from depression and loneliness to addictive behaviours, suicidal feelings, and difficulties in relating to others.

Why it is so hard to face sexual abuse

It is the shame that people feel when they have been violated that makes the abuse so difficult to overcome.

It is shame that keeps Belinda from being able to form close relationships with women and eliminates all but essential contact with men. Belinda is living in shame because she feels that, because she has been abused, she is now somehow tarnished. She believes that, as a "flawed" person, if someone got to know her they would not want to be her friend – and even if they did, once they discovered her past they would quickly reject her.

This is true of so many survivors like Belinda, who live in dread of other people discovering their abuse. The fear is that if people find out you have been abused, they will feel differently towards you – perhaps their perception of you and your sexuality will be distorted. It is this anxiety about being exposed that keeps survivors away from deep relationships – and isolates them.

It's about sex

Sexual abuse is also shameful because it is about the dark, destructive side of sex, which people do not feel comfortable with. Although our world is saturated with pictures, films, and books about sex, and many pubs and clubs are full of boasting and sexual innuendo, very few people really feel safe talking about their personal sexuality or their bodies – let alone about a painful abuse that has occurred. This leads to even more feelings of being alone with the problem and feeling that no one really understands what you are going through.

Other criminal offences that happen to people, such as being burgled or being mugged, just don't carry the same consequences as sexual assault because they are not related to our sexuality, which is so personal. It is relatively easy to tell others that you have had your handbag stolen; it is very different to say you have been raped.

Talking about it

Despite all the self-help books and TV confession shows that surround us, many adults have difficulty acknowledging that the wounds inflicted on them as children still have a profound effect on them as adults. Yet when we start communicating with others and breaking the silence around abuse, the pain does lessen.

I have been amazed by how, once I started to take the risk of talking about my past, my sense of isolation immediately started to melt away. I have also found that you can draw a strong feeling of compassion and strength from other people who may be on the same journey of healing as you are.

Group thinking

As well as looking for a counsellor (or perhaps instead of this) you may like to consider getting in contact with a Survivors service, a twelve-step group, which specializes in offering support to people who have experienced sexual abuse, or a rape and sexual abuse support centre which facilitates groups for survivors of sexual abuse.

If a Survivors group or support group is working well, it will have a strong sense of unity and purpose. You can often find hugely meaningful and significant support in the shared experience these groups provide. Also, unlike one-to-one therapy, they are a more democratic form of receiving support – all members are there to give and receive. You get the benefit of six people's input and not just one. They can be very comforting as well as very challenging. Also, the experience of just belonging to a group can be very healing, especially in Western culture where there is so much individualistic behaviour and thinking.

However, if you don't want to talk about your abuse or don't feel the people around you are trustworthy enough, then please don't let this book pressurize you! It is your choice.

Checkout sheet: Chapter one

. . . .

1. Did you realize that sexual abuse was so prevalent? How does that make you feel?

2. If you are not from the UK, do you suspect it could be the same in your own nation? How freely is sexual abuse acknowledged in your culture?

3. Have you told anyone that you've been abused?

4. What was their response? Were they supportive?

5. What did you want them to say?

6. What would you have said if you were them?

CHAPTER TWO

SHAME: THE BLAME GAME

Chloe's family were extremely close to another family in the small Polish village where she grew up. When she reached her teenage years she noticed the father of the other family was paying her a lot of attention. One day, when she was thirteen, they were alone together and he molested her. After swearing her to secrecy he started shouting at her, telling her she made him do it. Chloe was so devastated by what had happened that she did not talk about the incident for six years. Inside, the shame began to eat away at her. She became unable to form relationships or pursue a career and developed an eating disorder that left her dangerously overweight. Chloe had internalized her abuser's shame – the shame that did not belong to her.

Why we feel ashamed of something that is not our fault

If you have been sexually abused you will almost certainly experience intense feelings of shame about what has happened to you. This is partly because of society's attitude towards crimes of a sexual nature. Because abuse is a taboo topic, it is very difficult to find the right place to talk about it.

But there is another more sinister angle to the shame of abuse. In her book *Rescuing the Inner Child*, child therapist Penny Parks says this:

> The aggressor projects the blame and guilt onto the
> child and the child accepts that projection as truth. It
> is like life imprisonment for a crime that someone else
> has committed.[1]

Patti was sexually abused by her grandfather but neither she nor the rest of her family will admit it. Patti has been labelled by her family as a troublemaker and is now shunned and excluded by them. This is because she represents what they cannot face: the family shame. Patti has now internalized this shame and feels worthless and dirty.

It is almost as though the victims of the abuse, like Patti, actually carry the guilt that really belongs to the person who abused them. There is a very good reason for this: most perpetrators of abuse, like Patti's grandfather, do not admit the abuse happened, or if they do they are unwilling to take responsibility for their actions. This is particularly true for victims of abuse who have experienced some bodily pleasure during the abuse.

The victim is then left feeling that, in some strange way, they only have themselves to blame for what has happened, even though logically they know this cannot be the case. But it is this intense feeling of shame that will keep you from seeking help.

Abusers rely on the almost always correct perception that the victim will not break their silence. This then leaves the abuser free to carry on the abuse either with that victim or another, free from prosecution for their crime. They may achieve this through aggressive warnings like, "Tell anyone about this and something worse will happen to you"; or by using more subtle tricks such as telling their victim, "This is our special little secret – let's keep this between ourselves." More often than not, however, nothing is actually said during or after the act. The child may not be able to understand what

NEW SHOES

has happened in terms of sexuality, but instinctively knows that it is very wrong and that to talk about it is going to cause a lot of trouble.

Society has to a certain extent woken up to the alarming statistics about abuse. But there is still so much disbelief that ordinary people – parents, teachers, members of religious organizations, and authority figures – can actually be child abusers. If a child does try to seek help they run the risk of not being believed or, even worse, being punished for speaking out. The child is then engulfed by even more shame at having made a so-called false accusation.

Unfortunately this attitude often does not alter as children grow into adults. If a victim starts dealing with the abuse in adulthood and tries to voice their feelings, they will probably be met with blank faces and defensive responses from the members of the community or family involved. The victim will often be blamed, accused, and even completely ostracized, leaving them to shoulder the blame – and, of course, once again they will be alone.

A shameful act is given a shameful response, and the person involved is left with no choice but to absorb all the shame internally. But what is shame and why is it so devastating?

At its root, shame is a core feeling that we have about ourselves. Many people confuse shame with guilt, but they are in fact very different.

Guilt is about what we do, but shame is about who we are.

Guilt

Guilt is actually a very positive emotion. True guilt shows us when we have done something that is unwise and damaging to ourselves or others. When we feel guilt there is a way out, and that is to change our behaviour and sometimes to ask for forgiveness from anyone we have hurt.

Guilt enables us to learn from our experiences: make a different choice and the guilt will disappear. However, shame can never be resolved by behaviour because it is a permanent internal feeling and not based on external actions – and its effects are devastating.

If you try to have a conversation with Chloe you are going to have a hard time. Chloe has been so filled with shame during her childhood that now when people talk to her she looks up and down and to the side; she simply does not have the confidence to look another human being in the eye.

How shame enters

No one is born feeling ashamed. Shame enters a person during their childhood through significant relationships in that person's life.

There are three main ways that this happens:

1. Abandonment and rejection

When a child is physically left by a parent – the parent walks out of the home, or has an illness, or even dies – this can cause the child to feel shame. This is because children are very self-centred and assume that what is happening around them relates to them directly. They will then interpret the fact that "Mummy's left" as being something to do with Mummy not liking them. They don't have the resources to comprehend that Mummy leaving is about much wider issues in the home: they need support to be able to understand this.

Alternatively the child can be rejected by the parent on an emotionally more subtle level – the parent can't or won't connect with the child. This could be because the parent is very busy or pre-occupied with their own problems.

Arun's mother had three jobs to keep the family financially stable as her husband was too ill to work. Arun and his three brothers rarely saw her and certainly didn't have quality time with her. Without a father to give them any attention either, all four boys grew up feeling rejected by their parents.

2. Abuse
Shame also enters a child's life when that child is physically, emotionally, or sexually abused. This is also true if there is violence in the family – even if the child is not the one being physically abused. The fact that it is happening in the home will bring a sense of shame on the child.

3. Misnaming
When a child is called names by parents or other children or treated in a negative and undervaluing way, this can also make the child feel ashamed. Lola was overweight as a child, and at school and at home she was called "fatty", "porky" and "ugly". Finding it hard to concentrate on her studies and under such pressure in the playground, she constantly failed in her grades and exams. The way she was treated by her teachers and her parents also gave her the negative message she was stupid. Both the name-calling and the message that she was a failure were extremely damaging. They caused her a great deal of shame throughout her childhood and her adult years. This continued even after she had slimmed down to a regular size and through night classes achieved an education to degree standard.

Shame lives on
The child that is shamed can begin to live in a sense of shame. The shame stays inside the child and becomes a central part of their personality, so that by the time they reach adulthood much of their identity is built on this shame-filled foundation.

There was a ring on my doorbell recently at 7 a.m. on a Saturday morning and I instinctively knew who it was. I live in a badly insulated apartment and have a three-year-old who likes jumping up and down and shouting a lot! However, I was not prepared for the onslaught of abuse I received from my neighbour downstairs as I stood in the chilly February breeze in my nightie. "The noise upstairs is constant," he moaned. "All I hear is her noise and screaming. It's seven o'clock in the morning and I'm tired... you're the parent... Can't you control your child and stop her making so much noise?" I'm sure you can guess the rest.

Afterwards, as I closed the door, I analysed what I felt and decided it was shame. Looking back at the situation later, I realized that although he had the right to make his request for a quiet lie-in, the way he did it was totally unacceptable.

More than that, though, the shame I felt about the situation was not actually mine, but his.

The bitter fruits of shame

Shame is one of the most unhelpful emotions you can experience.

To live in shame is to live in a world of destructive internal dialogue and to perceive that others think this negatively about you too. It can also mean you are extremely self-conscious, and this negative self-awareness fills all of your thoughts and actions. You may feel there is something intrinsically wrong with you, and that other people will also find you somewhat unattractive and undesirable. These powerful feelings can spill into many different areas of your life, such as relationships, career, self-image, and how you think others see you.

Much of your day can be filled with destructive thoughts and feelings.

How shame comes out

Shame is about exposure and requires the presence of another person to be truly felt. That is why shame-filled people (like Chloe) can often display outward signals of shame and may be unable to look a person in the eye – they will find this kind of personal contact just too exposing.

Shame can lead to some very negative behaviour patterns, including:

Perfectionism
Shame makes us perfectionists. We try to get everything right in an inhuman way, covering every area of our lives so that no one will be able to criticize us.

Defensiveness
Shame-filled people can be very defensive and can't take any kind of criticism, even if it is constructive and helpful.

Isolation
Shame-filled people are very isolated, not wanting to get close to anyone in case the other person discovers too much about them.

Self-hatred
Shame-filled people are not happy with themselves, because their whole lives are crowded out by self-hatred and negative talk.

It is as though the shame seeps through and infiltrates your whole life.

Take some time to read the following list and tick any that you can relate to:

- Feeling "something is wrong with me"
- Fearing rejection by others when there is nothing to fear
- Feeling isolated and lonely – fearful of close relationships
- Fearing intimacy – wanting relationship but pushing people away

- Controlling of others – not letting go in relationships
- Being defensive and self-righteous – not accepting any criticism
- Exhibiting people-pleasing behaviour patterns – not aware of how to get your own needs met
- Punishing self with negative talk or even physical harm
- Feeling overly responsible for everyone and everything that happens
- Having an addictive personality – acting out behaviours such as over-eating, drinking, drug abuse
- Feeling depressed and sad

If you have ticked several of these points, try not to feel overwhelmed. Being able to identify the areas you need to work on is a really good sign and the first step in making changes.

Families characterized by shame

We will look at families in more detail in chapter five, but it is worth noting that families whose relationships are characterized by shame often deny or minimize the needs of the individuals in the family in order to protect the image the family projects both to its members and to the outside world.

Anyone who touches on an issue that could bring shame on the family is not tolerated. So, if a family member is aware that there are problems in the home and wants to seek help, they are not allowed. Or if an individual is feeling hurt by another family member, they are not allowed to express this. Rules are then formed around not having feelings or needs. For example, if you make a demand on another person that causes them some stress, you may be told, "You've upset your mother – this is all your fault!" It's almost as though the shame is passed around the family so that the person who is least able to protect themselves carries the family shame.

Internal anger and shame

Shame is also about anger. The anger is often directed towards yourself, for feeling that you have failed. When Libby's father walked out, Libby's mother blamed her and her sister, saying, "It was all going fine until we had kids." Libby grew up feeling shame and anger against herself for causing her mum so much pain. So when, twenty years later, her husband had an affair, it was Libby who apologized to him for being an inadequate wife and mother! This was a great relief to her husband but clearly left Libby filled with even more self-blame and anger.

Results of living in shame

If you feel constantly ashamed, the chances of you having a healthy lifestyle are low. Most people who live in shame are very lonely, as they are unable to form relationships or trust people because of the fear of exposure. This is a very dangerous place to be. Living in isolation leaves you open to trying to get rid of your emotions through addiction to alcohol, drugs, sex, or TV – anything that numbs your feelings. This obviously does not solve the problem, although it does give some temporary respite from the pain.

But is there another way out from years of living in shame? Is it possible to regain your sense of self after you have been so violated? Can you reverse the years of damage to relationships that shame has condemned you to?

I believe you can, and the rest of this chapter contains some ideas that I have found helpful both personally and professionally for those on the journey towards being free.

Talk about it!

The shame of abuse will often live on until it is brought out into the open and shared in a supportive environment.

Shame is about being isolated and fearing that people are going to reject you. Talking about your feelings will help you to reach a place of reality. The way to keep the shame going is to keep it to yourself and live a life of internal turmoil. Don't make that mistake. The very areas we do not want to talk about are often the issues we need to talk about most. If you have a close friend or partner whom you can open up to, that is all to the good.

However, in some situations the best place to share your fears is in the counselling room or within a support group.

Give it back

Putting the shame firmly back where it belongs in your own mind – even if that person never admits it – is part of the way to freedom.

This is not easy, but it is an essential part of recovery. Letter-writing is one way of doing this. Writing your thoughts down makes them more tangible and can help you to lift the false responsibility that you carry onto the abuser, where it belongs. However, a word of warning: undertaking a letter-writing exercise can provoke very powerful feelings. I would recommend you do not do this without the support of a close friend or preferably a counsellor.

Write a comforting letter to an imaginary child or young person who is around the age that you were when the abuse started, assuring the child that the abuse was not their fault. This can help you to connect with yourself as you were at that age and experience a fresh understanding of how vulnerable a child is. If this is hard to do, then think about a friend you were close to when you were that age. Picture that child in your mind: their size, their smile, their eyes, and their giggle.

Here are some ideas you could include in the letter:

- Assure the child they have done nothing wrong and have nothing to be ashamed of
- Explain why they are not to blame
- Specify why the abuser is the guilty party
- Would you like to touch or hug them? Can you say that in your letter?
- How could you give them permission to be angry and upset?
- Tell the child you feel sad and upset that they have suffered so cruelly
- Assure them you will look after them in the future
- How do you feel towards that child? Can you express it in writing?

You can write this letter as many times as you need to. It is interesting to do this over time and see how your perceptions change. This can be especially powerful if you have children yourself or are close to children, as this is a living example of their innocence and vulnerability.

Write a letter to the abuser

Write a letter with a view to naming the abuser as the person who is wholly responsible for the abuse. Again, please do this exercise with the support of someone else. I would add that you should not send this letter, no matter how tempting it may be in the heat of the moment. It could be an action you later regret.

Here are some ideas you might like to include:

- Tell the abuser you have carried their shame but you are now giving it back

- If the abuser silenced you by making you promise not to tell anyone, tell them you are now breaking that promise
- Hold the abuser solely responsible for the abuse
- If the abuser gave you sweets/affection/money or anything else in exchange for sex, then this is a double crime and they should be doubly ashamed
- Hold the abuser accountable for spoiling the self-image of a precious and unique child or young person[2]

List the choices you had as a child

Many people remember the abuse they suffered through the lenses of how they would respond to it now as an adult. They imagine that the choices they had as children are the same as the ones available to them now. But as a child your choices are very limited. Children are largely at the mercy of the adults in their lives and have to rely on them for help. If an adult does not respond to their cry there is very little they can do.

Imagine that a traumatic situation has just happened to you. Someone has attacked you in your own home. What are your choices?

- Call the police, in the expectation that they will believe you and work with you to press charges
- Get support from friends – possibly stay with them
- In the worst case scenario, move house

What choices would you have as a child in that same situation?

- Calling the police may not be possible and you may not be believed
- Friends at school would not be able to help you
- You cannot leave the house – you are trapped in the situation

Imagine a small child

Imagine a small child standing in front of you who has told you they have been sexually abused. It could be you; but if that is too much of a reach, imagine another child you may know, either now or in the past.

This child's name is ....

He /she is ....years old

He/she has ....eyes
and ....hair

This child has been sexually abused and is going to be looked after by another adult. You are now going to hand the child over to that adult.

How would you advise them to look after this child? What could you say to this adult to help them support and care for this child?

This child has been badly hurt by ....

This child needs ....

Please tell this child ....

Please do not tell this child ....

This child is innocent because ....

This child must have ....

This child deserves ....

Intention

Victims of sexual abuse and rape often look back at the situation and think, "I could/should have done something," or, "I should have told someone," or, "I should never have let it go on so long." Sexual abuse, however, is all about intention. You may have had to make choices because it was in your best interest to do so at that time. However, you need to clarify in your own mind, right from the start of the abuse, what your intention was and what the abuser's intention was. It is important to remember this even though exchanges may have taken place. This could have been exchanges of sweets, affection, or money; but as a child or young person your intentions were never about sexually gratifying an adult. Your life choices were extremely limited.

Some questions you might like to consider could be:

- Critically, who had the real power in that situation?
- Who originally initiated things?
- What was your fundamental motive as a child when you met this person?
- What was the abuser's primary motive?
- Who was leading?
- Who was being led?
- Did you do things just to "get it over with"?
- If this person gave you affection, did you get much attention elsewhere?
- If you accepted sweets or money, did you really understand what was happening? And what the price would have to be for you?
- If you could have told someone, who realistically would have helped you?

Join a support group

It can take a lot of courage, but as previously mentioned, joining a support group or survivors group can be pivotal in breaking shame. Speaking out your fears and receiving acceptance from others can break the secrecy in which shame thrives.

Time after time when I have run groups for survivors of sexual abuse, people have said to me, "Just to walk into the room and see other people who look just like me has helped me feel less alone and so much less ashamed." Such is the power of mutual support and community.

Look out for bad language!

Try to stop misnaming yourself. We can play negative messages over and over in our heads – for example, saying to ourselves, "I'm so stupid, I'll never get anything right," when we make a mistake. We need to take action against this, recognize when it is happening, and try some self-intervention to replace the negative messages with positive ones. There is an Old Testament proverb that says, "As a man thinks so he is." This is so true. If we constantly think we are going to mess up, the pressure is likely to make that a self-fulfilling prophecy.

Thinking positive thoughts about ourselves is far more likely to mean there is going to be a positive outcome. We will look at how to do this further in chapter four.

Checkout sheet: Chapter two

. . . .

1. Do you feel in any way to blame for the abuse you have suffered?

2. Why do you think this is?

3. If you read about a child being abused, would you consider them to blame?

4. Could you use any of the exercises in this chapter to help put the blame back onto the abuser?

5. Make a list of positive messages you could write down to remind yourself on a daily basis of your value.

CHAPTER THREE

MEMORIES: NOT SO EASY TO LEAVE THEM?

I stared at the credit card statement that lay unopened on the mat. Not wanting to view its contents, I stepped on it defiantly with my fabulous new designer UGG boots. There was of course a strong link between the two!

Living a truthful life means being committed to being honest and seeing reality as it is. However, facing the truth can be very painful and this is the reason why so many people choose not to face their difficulties but to carry on living in denial.

The consequence of this is that, just like an ever-increasing credit card statement, the problems do not go away; they escalate.

Research shows that many abused people bury the memory of the abuse they have suffered for many years. In Briere and Conte's study of a sample of 468 clinical subjects with sexual abuse histories, 279 (59.6 per cent) reported a period of their lives before the age of eighteen when they had been amnesic of their abuse.[1] This is because the truth of the abuse was so traumatic they could not face it. So people choose to live in denial about what has happened to them. But what exactly is denial? How does it work?

Denial

Denial is defined as a "refusal to acknowledge an unacceptable truth or emotion or to admit it into consciousness, used as a defence mechanism".[2] Living in denial is very understandable when what you have to face is so horrific. When we step out of denial we face the reality of our lives. This may mean facing the fact that we were abused and coming to terms with the damage it has done. We may hate the truth at first, but facing the trauma is ultimately the way out of the hidden pain of the past.

Anita is in unconscious denial about her abuse. If you were to ask her if she had been abused she would say no, but her body says something different. Anita's memory shockingly resurfaced when she went into the doctor's surgery for her first smear test. She became very distressed when the procedure began, and the nurse involved became so concerned for her she advised her to seek psychological help.

Facing the truth of buried pain

Children, especially those who have been abused by a trusted relative or friend, simply cannot cope mentally with the pain of what has happened. In order to carry on living their lives in some kind of order, they push the trauma into their subconscious and often it can lie hidden away for years. But its effects can be seen in damaged, unhappy lives, and the problems resurface, especially in relationships.

Other effects of abuse can include:

- Lack of trust in people and possibly God (if you have a faith)

- Feeling fearful for no reason

- Feeling shameful without knowing why

- Hating yourself and your own body

- Self-harming – for example, cutting yourself

- Feeling suicidal

- Addictive behaviours – dependence on drugs or alcohol or compulsive eating

- Feeling extremely angry, particularly with authority figures or with those of the same sex as your abuser
- Feeling disconnected from others
- Feeling incredibly anxious
- Feeling numb – not really feeling much at all, whether good or bad
- Having sexual problems
- Feeling generally that your life is not going well

Once faced, however, abuse can still be very difficult to come to terms with and we can enter into a different kind of denial about the damage we have suffered.

Have you ever had thoughts along these lines?

- Denied feelings: "I was never abused and even if I was it didn't do me any harm."
- Minimized feelings: "I do feel pain sometimes, but it was years ago so it doesn't matter any more."
- Trivialized feelings: "I have been abused, but so have a lot of people. It's no big deal."

Perhaps the most beneficial way to respond to these thoughts is through:

- Embracing feelings: "Yes, I've been abused and the pain is very real. But it is only by facing it that I can progress with my life and move away from it."

Our response to the abuse will affect our ability to recover from it. If we do not confront the reality of the abuse and its damage, we are impaired in our healing.

Fantasy and spacing out

Like other forms of abuse, being sexually abused is extremely traumatic for a child – especially if it is ongoing. In order to cope with what is happening, some children mentally dissociate from the abuse.

Dissociation takes a wide range of forms. At one end of the spectrum a person may find themselves entering a daydream world or even "getting lost", as you would in a book or at the cinema, where you lose touch with your immediate surroundings. At the other end, there are dissociate disorders such as Dissociative Identity Disorder (DID), which can result in a serious inability to function in relationships and life.

DID is a separate and important issue, but is not one that can be addressed in this particular book. If you think you may be struggling with DID then you need to get professional help from a counsellor or health worker who can support you.

In this book we are going to look at people at the lower end of the spectrum – people who dissociate by escaping into an internal fantasy world. This fantasy world is a way of mentally or emotionally leaving the situation so that the connection with the present pain is temporarily lost. It is a self-protective coping mechanism used by many victims of abuse to make a horrific situation bearable. This is because the fear of their situation is so great that mentally they cannot bear to stay in it. A fantasy life anaesthetizes these painful feelings. This means that during the abuse or distressing time, the victim will be able to switch off; part of their mind will not be there, having escaped into another world.

The problem with fantasy is that it doesn't just end when the abusive situation finishes. It has addictive and obsessive characteristics and is difficult for the victim to let go of.

Fantasy is very different from a pleasant daydream or even an exciting vision of how you want your life to be. Daydreams or visions can actually propel you forward towards your goals, but a fantasy is just an escape from your present life and does nothing for your future, because it will never become a reality.

As someone who was sexually abused for many years, I developed a strong fantasy life. It was a very useful coping mechanism that allowed me to escape from the dreadful reality of my situation. I would mentally remove myself from my present and let my mind drift to a far-away dreamland where I was safe and secure and no one could hurt me. However, what works for a girl of twelve who is a repeated victim of abuse does not work for a woman of thirty-six who is trying to build a communicative marriage.

At times of conflict and stress I often withdraw into my own world. This leaves those close to me feeling that although I am physically present, I have emotionally left. I am sure you can imagine that even though (I am so thankful to say) I have a very patient and loving husband, there are times when our relationship is under considerable strain because I can be very distant and he feels extremely alone.

It is not only your relationships that suffer when you escape into a fantasy world. My friend (and fellow survivor) Lynn noticed that throughout her education she would often find it extremely difficult to stay focused and listen to teachers or lecturers – and her work suffered as a result. We discussed this together and both decided we needed to address the issue before our lives slowly seeped away into our own internal fantasy world.

A fantasy test
Think back over the past week and ask yourself the following questions. Also, ask people close to you if they think any of these points could apply to you:

- When you are with people, are you present mentally?
- Do you listen, and remember what is said?
- Do you often find your mind drifting off somewhere else?
- Do people ever comment to you that you seem far away and distant?
- Has anyone commented that you are hard to access emotionally?

Of course, everyone has times when there are things on their mind and they can't give others their full attention. But if this becomes a pattern, it can lead to a very isolated lifestyle in which people feel unable to connect with you. As in Lynn's case, fantasy can also make it very difficult to work, as concentration can be impaired, and it can be hard to listen to teachers or work colleagues for any length of time. This obviously leads to low grades and a low work achievement.

Here are some other negative implications of fantasy:

- It can become a lifestyle or pattern
- It is isolating and relationships suffer due to lack of intimacy
- It leads to imaginary thinking and unrealistic expectations
- It reduces attention span and makes learning extremely difficult
- It can limit growth and change

Overcoming fantasy

Having my friend Lynn in my life was a real help for me, as she understood exactly what I was going through and was able to recognize when I was drifting off into my own world. Often, being accountable to a friend or counsellor is a key way to break out of the fantasy cycle. But even if you don't have a friend who can support you, it is still possible to make breakthroughs in this area.

The first step is to face the root of the problems that cause you to fantasize. This means beginning to face the pain of the past. To do this, you may need to enter into counselling. It is important to understand where your fantasy stems from and why you entered into it originally. Next try to gauge the key moments when you are likely to become distant from others or your surroundings.

- Is it when you are bored?
- Is it at a moment of intimacy?
- Is it when you are feeling anxious?
- Does stress affect your behaviour?

Write this down or mentally note it, and next time boredom kicks in, try to catch yourself when you sense you are beginning to switch off. Here are some steps you can try:

- Physically moving can be a way of helping to bring yourself into the present.
- Speak up or change the subject to get yourself into a conversation if you are sitting outside it or beginning to retreat into your own world.
- If you are in a lecture or lesson, begin writing down what is said, as this will start to occupy your mind instead of the fantasy.
- Discuss the fantasies and obsessions with someone you trust. Do they indicate any legitimate needs in your current life? For example: Do you long for more closeness in relationships but think you will only be able to have them in your daydreams? How could you help yourself make that happen in reality instead of just in your head? What support do you need to get here?

• •

Facing the memories

The reason we need to look back at the abuse is not so that it can haunt us, but so that we can reclaim the part of ourselves that became damaged when it happened. By identifying the root cause of our behaviour, we can free ourselves to grow and not just change our outward behaviour patterns. It is not what happened that counts, but the traumatic impact it had on us. That is why we go back to investigate those memories.

It will also help us to have a firm handle on our past, because at times memories from the past can suddenly intrude on our lives in the present.

Why memories are blocked

Many people who have suffered sexual abuse as children find the area of remembering very difficult. Often events have been so traumatic that part or all of the details of what happened are repressed. Not being able to remember is a self-protective mechanism – the trauma of being abused by someone you may have loved and trusted is too much to cope with mentally. This is especially true if you were put under extreme pressure by the abuser. Repression and denial are logical ways of surviving – you had to find some way of containing the information.

Most victims say there are blocks on their memory. For some nearly everything is blocked; others can remember much more.

It is also the case that memories are kept alive by repetition. We all have funny stories that we bring out in the company of those who witnessed them. We will say, "Do you remember the time ten years ago when we thought we were on the train to Manchester and it turned out to be the train to Sheffield...?" These stories are kept alive by others affirming and repeating them. This is extremely unlikely to happen with abuse. You are unlikely to have the memory of being abused confirmed by anyone except the abuser. Others may be able to remember the circumstances surrounding the abuse, which can be helpful. However, although the impact of what happened may not fade, the actual memory often does.

Memories also vary enormously. For instance, if you kept your eyes closed during the abuse, you will not have any visual memories of it. But certain smells or tastes may bring back strong feelings that remind you of what happened.

Memories surface in different ways and can intrude into our current lives. The reason why we look at our memories is so that they can no longer control us. It can be very disturbing to suddenly have a strong feeling or picture in your mind and not know where it comes from.

There are several different types of memories:

Recall memory
This is the normal way of remembering: you recall the event and the emotions it produced. It is a complete memory.

Imagistic memory
These are snapshot memories that come up very suddenly and then are gone again. They can be triggered by something in your environment, such as a perfume, or a sound that your subconscious recognizes, which then emerges into your conscious mind in picture form.

Feeling memory
Feeling memories are triggered by something or someone. They often register as an extreme response to a situation or a person, and can make you feel very out of control. You may experience a feeling of anxiety or anger without being able to anchor it in an actual event.

When June moved into her new apartment she couldn't understand why she experienced a strong feeling of fear every time she went into the bathroom. Then one day it clicked: the wallpaper in the bathroom was exactly the same as that of her bedroom where, as a child, she had been abused. June's subconscious had remembered something from the past and it had brought back all the feelings of anxiety. However, once June was able to root the feeling in a specific memory she had control over it.

Body memory

This is a physical feeling or response to what has happened, after the event – perhaps a feeling of nausea or repulsion or tightness in the body. A classic example of this is in the area of physical contact, when your body sends negative messages to your brain that put you back in touch with the abuse – as in the case of Anita's smear test. Through the smear test Anita had shockingly come into contact with the abuse that had festered in her subconscious for many years.

Acting out memory

This is a pattern of behaviour that is repeated, although you don't have any knowledge of what the root cause is. This could be constantly washing because you feel dirty, but not knowing where the feeling is coming from.

Mia's life was one long cycle of cleaning, washing, hoovering, and tidying up. Every day she toiled from when she awoke to when she went to bed, making sure there was not a speck of dirt in her house. She fitted her work and her friends around her cleaning schedule. Mia was "acting out" in her adult life her inner desire to be clean from her past. It wasn't until she began to seek help that she was able to go into a restaurant and order a cup of tea. Previously she had been a virtual prisoner to her obsession with hygiene, and drinking out of a cup she personally had not washed to her satisfaction would have caused her a near panic attack.

However, after some counselling sessions, she was able to go to restaurants and cafés with friends and start to rebuild her social life.

Reclaiming memory

Recovering memories has become a somewhat controversial subject, following negative publicity in the media regarding "False Memory Syndrome". This has led to some counsellors and therapists being accused of manipulating their clients into thinking they were abused as children. Perhaps the key thing to bear in mind here is that frantically searching for and forcing memories is not very helpful. Memories come up when we are ready to face them. Some memories may take many years to recover but will emerge in their own time. Sometimes, however, victims of abuse feel that if they can only remember the past clearly, it will be like a magic solution that will solve all their problems. However, this is rarely the case. Linking a memory may be helpful, as it was for June in her new apartment, but it does not instantly remove all the effects the abuse has had on our lives.

Recovering memories often begins with the process of unlocking emotions. For instance, you can ask yourself why certain people bring out strong feelings in you and who they remind you of from your past.

You also should be aware that uncovering memories may also unlock deep fears, insecurities, rage, and hurt and may even bring on panic attacks or depression which are linked with the feelings you may have buried.

You may need some extra support around that time. It may be helpful to plan how you can get support before that happens. For example, you could go to your doctor and ask for some counselling, or tell a best friend you are going through a very difficult time and ask them to be around for you. You can also make a special time daily to go to your "safe space".

There are other ways to get in touch with your memories:

- You could journal your feelings and trace patterns from today to your past.
- You could look at any childhood photos and see if you can spot any differences in expression in the photos.
- Talking to trusted friends and listening to anything they can remember of your life story is also a good way of rediscovering your past.

When you think of your childhood, what feelings does it provoke in you?

- Do you remember a time when your feelings dramatically changed?
- What would you like to change about your past? What would you like to enjoy or repeat?
- Were you able to express yourself freely to your family? To your friends? At school?
- Is there someone or somewhere in your life that enables you to be free to express yourself?
- Could you explore finding someone or somewhere?

Even if we do not always remember it clearly, the past does have a tremendous impact on the way we are today. Bringing it back to our minds can help us to understand some of our behaviours in the present, and therefore to move on from them if we so choose.

However, for most people not every aspect of their childhood was unhappy: there were times that were fun and positive. These times may well be worth repeating in our adult lives. It is my observation that survivors sometimes have a difficult time embracing fun and joy, and their lives have become quite dull. You may like to consider the following:

- What gifts and talents did you have as a child that you don't enjoy now – for example, painting or playing a sport or the guitar?
- Can you find a way of incorporating that into your life now even if it's only once a month?

Flashbacks

Some people may experience sudden memories or flashbacks which can be very upsetting. Flashbacks occur to people after they have experienced a traumatic incident: they are memories of that trauma that have not been processed yet. During abuse, memories of the incident are often kept inside in order to protect the victim from the horror of what is going on. These feelings remain locked inside until a "trigger" from the present releases the memory. When you experience flashbacks it can be as though you are experiencing the abuse again in the present, and you lose touch with reality. This can be extremely frightening.

One way you can help yourself to return to the present if you are experiencing a flashback is to practise "grounding" yourself. This means you are bringing yourself from your past memory into the here-and-now.

Grounding tips

Feet first
Put your feet firmly on the floor – stamp if you like – reminding yourself of the here-and-now.

Breathe
Be aware of your breathing. When we are fearful we can start to breathe very quickly. Take a few minutes to breathe in and out slowly. Count if that helps: four counts in, and six counts out.

Use your senses to bring you into today
Use your senses to bring you into the here-and-now.

- Look: take in the shapes, colours, people that are around you.
- Listen: to noises such as music, birds, people talking.
- Feel: touch and feel your hands, arms, legs, the furniture – all reminding you of where you are now.

Remind yourself
This is just a memory – this is not actually happening. The worst is over, so focus on who you are now. If it helps, talk to the frightened "child" part of you and assure them that you (your healthy adult self) can take care of them now.

Hold something
In a strong flashback it is easy to lose perspective, and even not to know where you end and the rest of the world begins. Holding a blanket round yourself or hugging a pillow can help.

Take time
Don't push yourself to do things after a flashback – be kind to yourself. If you can, do something you find comforting such as drinking a hot drink.

Get support
If you feel you would like to, let your friends know what you are going through and let them help you by talking to you, touching you – whatever helps to remind you of who you are now.

Write it down
Flashbacks feel frightening because they can seem to come out of nowhere. When you feel ready, write down the

flashback and what happened directly beforehand. This will help you to identify the "trigger" and will help you gain an understanding of where the memory came from.

Share it
Consider joining a self-help group or finding a good therapist to help you through this time.[3]

The good news about flashbacks
Although flashbacks are frightening, they mean that the memories are coming up for a reason. If flashbacks are only experienced again and again with no information attached they are very traumatizing, but often flashbacks come up because you are ready to talk through the memory.

This can be another very positive step towards growth and healing. Writing the flashback down and talking it through in counselling can enable the memory processing system to reintegrate the memory so that it becomes part of the healing process. After this has happened these memories can't suddenly "jump out at you" and you will feel much more in control of them – and indeed of your life.

If you are experiencing flashbacks, use the grounding techniques and then write down as much as you can remember about the flashback. With support, talk through this memory and what it might mean. The chances are you will not experience the same level of anxiety the next time this memory comes up.

Be encouraged – the past is losing its grip. You are moving on.

Checkout sheet: Chapter three

• •

1. Has anyone ever mentioned that they find you are "spaced out" or "not really there"?

2. Do you have a particular "scenario" that you return to again and again but maybe in a different storyline?

3. Can you root this fantasy in anything – for example, loneliness, anger, feeling unvalued?

4. Has a memory ever suddenly intruded into your life? How did you handle it?

5. Do you think the grounding technique could help you?

CHAPTER FOUR

ANGER: FADE TO RED

"I'm sorry. I haven't managed to fill in the tax credit form in time." My husband looked sheepish. I was in no mood for an apology. It was now the end of July and I had requested he fill out the form again and again since the beginning of April. He had constantly ignored my requests and as I had predicted it was now too late for the deadline. I walked out of the room and slammed the door. I was extremely angry.

Anger has, by and large, a very bad press.

Our media and our communities are filled with reports of atrocities committed by people filled with hate and rage: murder, rape, racism, and of course "road rage". People have actually been killed because another driver cannot control their emotions. But is this really true anger?

If we take a look at anger close up, we might be very surprised.

What is anger?
In Neil Warren's book *Make Anger Your Ally*, anger is described as a "physical state of readiness".[1] When we are angry adrenaline is secreted, our blood pressure rises, we are highly alert, and the pupils of our eyes open wide. When we are angry all the power hidden inside of us becomes suddenly available to us. This is anger: preparedness and power. Anger is not the actions people take because they are angry – this is the expression of anger and not anger itself.

Anger empowers us to fight for change

Anger is a powerful force. Locked inside, it can cause tremendous self-damage through depression and physical pain; out of control and externalized, it can cause violence and emotional damage to others. However, anger can also be positive: it can provide the motivation for change and healing.

If people did not become angry, our world would never change – in fact it would be a truly horrific place to live. Look at some of the great reformers of society: Martin Luther King, Nelson Mandela, Ghandi. They were all motivated by a feeling of injustice and anger at the oppression taking place in their world and decided to do something about it, at great personal cost.

But what is anger and why does it evoke such a powerful response in us?

We avoid anger

By and large in most communities and families in the UK, people rarely allow their anger to be articulated freely. In some cultures, however, anger is much more freely expressed. Often we are uncomfortable with anger, and underlying tensions lie unexpressed between people. This means that although someone might be very angry with another person, instead of confronting them, they simply withdraw from the relationship. This results in relationships in which people may be outwardly polite to each other but underneath they are distanced and unreal.

Anger is a secondary emotion

In many ways, anger is a feeling just like any other feeling. But the difference with anger is that it has the power to affect others dramatically, perhaps because it can often be used very destructively – as is often the case with road rage, for example. Anger is an intense feeling and can have frightening consequences – both for us and for those close to us – and that is why many people don't like experiencing it.

But anger is not a primary emotion – it is a secondary emotion. This means there is always something else behind it. This is clearly illustrated in a passage from *Wuthering Heights*[2] in which Heathcliffe says, "I'm trying to settle how I shall pay Hindley back... I hope he will not die before I do!" His companion responds by saying: "For shame, Heathcliffe! It is for God to punish wicked people; we should learn to forgive." Heathcliffe's reply is very telling: "No, God won't have the satisfaction I should have. I only wish I knew the best way! Let me alone, and I'll plan it out: while I am thinking of that I don't feel the pain."

Anger always has another emotion underneath it. I would class this as a feeling of pain. First we experience pain and then we feel anger. This may happen so quickly that we may be unaware of feeling pain at all. However, pain often comes from feeling disempowered in a situation or, with abuse victims especially, from feeling that our boundaries have been violated.

I must admit that when I get on a crowded train and someone pushes into me I do feel extremely angry. I can see that this is because in the past my boundaries have been violated, so being pushed instantly taps into my rage about the original abuse. Understanding where the anger comes from gives me some power not to respond as I have done in the past, which is by swearing at the person pushing me. This response does not give me what I want from the offending person, whereas talking directly to the person calmly may well do. I still have some way to go, however, as I often battle with the desire to push back!

I know from past experience that as I work through these painful feelings, my anger will dissipate and be resolved.

• •

Yet we should not expect to never feel angry. Anger is there to highlight that something has happened which needs addressing. It may take some time to find the core issue, but no one becomes angry for no reason at all.

Shani would never admit she is angry. She never raises her voice or slams a door in frustration. She sits silently tapping away at her computer as her boss continues to take advantage of her, making her work through her lunches and stay late when she has a young daughter to pick up from school. But Shani is quietly smouldering underneath, and her sharp comments tell other people to keep away. Her body language and attitude display her anger, but it's hard to place it because she always denies it. She is angry, but she won't own her anger and therefore she can't use it to empower her to change the situation by asking her boss to respect her and her boundaries.

Anger also has a frightening side. It is especially frightening if you have been surrounded by conflict, anger, and violence as a child, directed either at you or at another family member. On the other hand, anger is also frightening if there was no conflict openly expressed in your family, as it becomes a completely unknown quantity. Finally, but perhaps most importantly, anger is frightening when we see it in ourselves because when we tap into pools of unresolved anger, or rage, we often feel out of control and unsafe.

Anger and abuse

Abuse victims often appear outwardly placid and compliant, but inside they are filled with rage, hostility, and anger. This anger can be focused towards many different people:

- The abuser
- The non-offending parent or relative
- The society, church (or faith community), or school that allowed it to happen

Although this anger might not be recognized, it is often taken into other relationships. Someone today reminds you of someone else from your past, and all your angry feelings come out at that person rather than the person who originally hurt you. A classic example is when we become extremely angry with our partner, although they have done little to hurt us. It is almost as though the person in your present life is getting all the mail which should be addressed to the person in your past.

Dormant anger

Not all abused people recognize they are angry. Their anger is often repressed (or dormant) and manifests itself in different ways:

Repression

Repressed anger can manifest through depression, tiredness, or physical ailments.

Fantasy

Often in fantasies and daydreams we can express anger that we are too afraid to express in real life.

Transference

We can react angrily to certain people even though they may have done little to harm us. This is because someone in our present life reminds us of someone in our past, and we take out our resulting emotions on the wrong person.

Contempt and envy

Another way anger can manifest itself is through feelings of contempt towards others and towards ourselves. This provides the illusion of power. It stops us feeling the loneliness and shame of our situation, and deadens our desires for the things we desperately want. If we feel contempt for a situation or a person it will stop us from wanting that situation or person in our lives. But it will also prevent us from having meaningful relationships.

However, these needs do not go away easily. Although we may outwardly display disdain for a person or situation, and we may fool those around us and even ourselves, inwardly we are often envious of that person. Weddings are a common place to find envy and contempt mixed together, both in single people and in those whose marriages and relationships are going through a difficult phase. People may outwardly express scorn towards those getting married, but inwardly feel jealous and wish it was them. We experience envy when our real inward desires surface and we can't push them away.

There is another side to anger as well – and that is anger towards ourselves. Often people who have been sexually abused turn their anger inwards and it comes out as self-hatred.

Self-hatred: anger gone inside

Self-hatred or self-contempt manifests as a sense of unworthiness and of strong negative feelings towards ourselves. Usually this comes into play because we believe that if we blame ourselves, we will not have to look at who has caused us to feel the pain of the abuse in the first place.

Self-hatred is so damaging because it stops us from enjoying ourselves and the good things life can give us. It can become a thought pattern that plays over and over in our minds. We may not even realize it, but it builds up into a constant internal dialogue which we then transfer into the minds of others, so that "I'm stupid and ugly" becomes "He thinks I'm stupid and ugly".

Self-contempt varies from having suicidal desires to despising compliments. If you suffer from acute self-hate, not only can you enter into self-harming activities such as cutting yourself, you can even subconsciously endanger your life. Angie regularly walks home from parties in the middle of the night in a dangerous district – even accepting lifts from strangers. Angie is very self-contemptuous: she cares little for herself and deliberately puts herself in harm's way.

But even if you do not enter into such dramatic behaviour as Angie, if you do not like yourself, life is going to be very difficult for you.

People who do not respect themselves often have an extremely negative view of their appearance and have difficulty receiving gifts and support from others. For example, it may be very hard for them to receive a compliment; they may have an inability to relax and enjoy being themselves; and they may have many negative thought patterns. All of this will, of course, affect those around them and make it difficult for them to enter into close relationships.

The way out of self-hatred is to expose it and to work on replacing the negative messages with positive ones.

Exposing self-hatred

I had a counsellor once who made me wear an elastic band around my wrist for a week. Every time I said or thought something negative about myself – for example "Oh no! I've spilled my coffee. I'm such a dummy!" – I would have to flick the elastic band.

By the end of the week my wrist was quite sore. I had had no idea how many negative messages I was giving myself. No wonder I found life an effort! It is an exercise you may like to try yourself.

At the end of the week we both concluded that I needed to start working on this extremely disabling self-talk. It took a lot of practice, but inserting a positive message into my mind when I could have had a negative thought did actually begin to change my thinking.

• •

Here are some examples of positive self-talk:

- You made it on time – that was well planned
- You've done a good job
- You came across well at the party – people seemed to enjoy your company
- You look good in those jeans
- You were very tactful at work today
- You were late but you apologized and it was no big deal

There is only one you!

Sometimes it is hard to believe that there will never be another person like us, but it's true! Self-hatred takes away the love and respect we should have for ourselves and our bodies. It is also true that, if we hate ourselves, we will find it almost impossible to love and accept others, or to have them return those feelings.

The way out of contempt is to look at our thought patterns and try to find the fundamental reasons why we condemn ourselves. Ask yourself why you are giving yourself negative messages:

- Does that message come from you or someone else?
- Who said it and what was said?
- Is it because of the way you were treated?

Talk to a close friend if you can about your feelings

- What is their perspective?
- How would they describe you?

Ask several people – don't just stick to one.

This is a hard task for some people, but write down twenty things you like about yourself. Start small – for example,

"I'm good at parking" – and then build up to some bigger areas.

Hatred of others

Hatred of others is a protective mechanism which ensures that you avoid close or intimate relationships. This is because if the person who abused you was close to you and knew you well, somewhere in your subconscious you will relate intimacy to abuse. As a result, you may feel that intimacy must be avoided at all costs so that you will not be abused again. This can cause you to be very negative, and even rude towards people who may have done nothing to deserve it, which inevitably leads to behaviour patterns that are very isolating.

There is a classic scenario in many romantic comedies in which a man and woman's relationship begins with real animosity, but by the end of the film they are in each other's arms – if not married! This is not the case in real life, however. Most people just do not have the inner resources to cope with this kind of rejection. Outward derision towards others does not generally make you attractive and usually means you will stay in isolation, often finding it difficult to get work and not being popular socially. Or you may be tempted to take your contempt further, perhaps to offending others, either physically or verbally.

Veronica acts oddly around men she finds attractive. She often pokes fun at them and humiliates them in front of others. This ensures that they will never ask her for a date, and she does not have to risk a relationship with all the potential vulnerability that would entail. Veronica is making sure by her behaviour that she will always remain in control – but the price she is going to have to pay is remaining single.

• •

Anger uncontrolled

Rage is another more accentuated form of anger. Anger can be empowering and constructive, but rage is ultimately destructive. Taken to its extremes, rage turned outwards towards others becomes murderous, and turned inwards towards self becomes suicidal.

Rage is a pool of unresolved anger that has been building up for years. The expression "the straw that broke the camel's back" very appropriately describes what happens when we tap into that pool of rage. Something happens in your daily life and it taps in to other pockets of unresolved anger inside you. At this point you can inadvertently light the touch paper of your internal rage and end up paying a very bitter price for it.

One sad example of this is that of Maxine Breakspear, who had a long history of child abuse at the hands of men. At the age of just eighteen, when one more man became abusive, she simply snapped. She murdered him with a knife in what was described as "a ferocious attack" by the investigating police officer. "I took all my anger out on him," she said. "I should have got myself sorted out before it got to that but I had no idea how to help myself."[3] Maxine will be thirty-two before she is considered for release.

Like so many victims of violence, Maxine desperately needed help earlier and she wasn't able to get it. Working out our anger is so important because, although we may not end up in a situation as extreme as Maxine's, uncontrolled rage can cause untold damage in our lives and the lives of those around us.

Rage needs to be dealt with, but anger is an emotion we should expect to feel in this life. Our aim is to get rid of unresolved rage so that our anger is appropriate to the situation.

Get that anger out!

If you have been abused, much of what you may need to work on is getting your old anger out, whether it manifests itself in contempt or rage or self-hate. You will also need to work on placing your anger onto your abuser.

You may need to process your rage, which can be difficult, so you may need support to do this. Flying into a rage (which is the result of many years of pain and stress), or quietly smouldering like Shani, often means that others can dismiss your genuine needs along with your behaviour.

Write an angry letter

Try writing a letter to someone you feel angry with, but don't send it. As with the other letter-writing exercises, make sure you do this with support.

Writing down your anger can release your feelings and enable you to help put the shame of the abuse back where it belongs – even if you only write down short sentences such as "I HATE YOU", or swear words. These carry strength of feeling and can help you begin to release the inner rage held inside.

For some people, the thought of writing to their abuser is too overwhelming, so don't start with that. Write your first letter to someone who has recently caused you a more minor frustration or upset, such as a shop assistant who was rude to you or a friend who let you down.

You could state:

- What they did wrong
- How that made you feel
- The impact it had on you
- What they should have done
- How you would like to be treated in the future

Writing out your anger – any anger – is a really helpful way of starting to get anger out. Once you have done this, begin writing to other people who have also caused you damage and who should have protected you when you were a child. People you might want to consider are:

• Parents
• Other family members
• Teachers
• Your community
• Religious leaders
• Social workers
• Police
• Doctors or nurses
• Youth workers

When you are ready, turn your attention to writing to the abuser. Here are some ideas about what you could include in a letter:

• What the abuser has done to hurt you
• How they should have behaved
• How they have failed you
• The responsibility they carry
• How they have betrayed you
• The impact the abuse has had on your life
• A reminder to them that you are a valuable person who deserves respect

Writing out your anger is a way of processing the rage that is lying inside you. It lessens the possibility that your anger will suddenly jump out of you when you're not expecting it.

Processing our rage means that the anger we feel today will be relevant to our current situation, and this means we will be more likely to be taken seriously.

Go swimming!

Sometimes feelings of anger can be so intense you feel like screaming. But if like many people you live in close proximity to others, you will need to find somewhere else to do it. A swimming pool (preferably with a slide!) can be the ideal venue. Swimming pools are often so noisy that you can shout and even scream without other people looking at you suspiciously. A ride on a rollercoaster could also be a good place to try this.

Getting anger under control

Des and Lily loved each other but both came from violent backgrounds. Their arguments were becoming more and more out of control. Their voices were getting louder and the language they used was becoming more threatening. After Lily threw her mobile phone at the wall in frustration, they both agreed they needed to get help. It was a wise decision. They had not waited until one of them had got physically hurt.

In the counsellor's room they both began to realize the impact that the violence they had witnessed in the past was having on their relationship. But understanding their past was not enough – they needed help in their relationship now. With the counsellor's help they both agreed and put into action a "Time Out" plan. This may sound like something that "Supernanny" would enforce on naughty children, but it is actually a powerful technique for de-escalating situations before they become dangerous.

A Time Out plan works in a situation of conflict. You are in a fight with your partner and you begin to notice the signals of anger. Physically these could include:

- Tightening of the chest
- Reddening of the face
- A churning stomach
- Tearfulness
- Sweating
- Pointing with fingers

You also start to discern a change in your language:

- It is getting more provocative
- You are getting louder
- You have started name-calling
- You are swearing at your partner

Once you spot these signals, agree with your partner that you both need to take a break. Agree a specific period for a Time Out; for example, twenty minutes. You will then separate for twenty minutes – it is best to separate physically and leave the room.

Agree that you will meet again in twenty minutes, and you must both stick to this, otherwise next time you call a Time Out your partner might not trust you to return.

Time Outs are very useful if you are going through a lot of pressure in your relationship. Creating the space in a Time Out means that when you come back together to talk (as Des and Lily did), you will feel calmer and more in control, and both of you are likely to get a better result. It also encourages safety in the relationship and helps to build trust between the couple.

Expressing it well
Does the way you express your anger get you what you want? Does it help you to be taken seriously and get the respect you

deserve? Certainly slamming the door on my husband when he had not filled in the tax credit form did not get it sent off any quicker. In addition, we may need to look at whether our anger is relevant to the situation we are facing. Perhaps you could think of this as "clean anger".

We may need to take the following steps in order to do this:

- Notice the signals that you are beginning to feel angry – for example, reddening of face

- Use this as a warning that something is about to happen

- If you are able, remove yourself from the situation to give yourself time to think

- If not, take some deep breaths and focus on your breathing for a few seconds

- Try to think long-term. This is especially important if you are prone to flying off the handle. Think through your options. "If I say this, I may feel better for the next five minutes but will I regret it in an hour or a week?" Ask yourself, "Am I hurting myself by doing something now that I will later wish I hadn't?"

- Write down your feelings at the time or as close to the incident as possible. This could just be single words, such as: angry, furious, frustrated, unheard, hurt, rejected.

- Try to remember if you have experienced this feeling before and where. Has your current situation triggered something from your past?

- Notice any patterns of feelings

- Could your current situation be tapping into a past circumstance? For example: "My boss constantly overlooks me for promotion" could link to "I was never really valued by my father". Who is it you are really angry with? Yes, your boss is not acknowledging your efforts, but in many ways this feels like a repeat of the way your dad treated you.

- With that in mind, is your anger appropriate to the situation?
- What do you want from the situation?
- How could you ask for this in such a way that you are likely to be heard?
- If this person can't give you this, is there anyone else who can give you support?

This will also help us to be assertive without being aggressive. As a result, we will have better, more open relationships in which we can express our feelings and desires to others in a way that they will find easier to respond to.

Checkout sheet: Chapter four

1. How do you feel now when people are angry with you or around you?

2. What do you feel when you get angry? Where can you feel the anger in your body – is it in your chest or head?

3. Have you ever transferred your anger onto an innocent person?

4. Do you think implementing a Time Out policy could be helpful for you and your partner?

5. Has anyone paid you a compliment recently? How did you respond? Did you believe what they said was true?

CHAPTER FIVE

GROWING UP: IT'S A FAMILY AFFAIR

So much has been written in the last twenty years about families and yet we cannot overestimate the impact our original families have on our lives. Families are the door to our world. Doors open both ways, and how you experience life now as an adult largely depends on how you experienced life at home as a child and how those around you treated you and each other.

When there is abuse in a family, we don't just focus on the abuse – this is often just the tip of the iceburg. The family system which led to the abuse being allowed to happen needs investigating. The home of an abused child is often harsh, controlling, and emotionally negligent. Children accept the abusive situation they are in because they have nothing to compare it with; and they sometimes go on to repeat this familiar (although horrific) situation in adulthood by transferring their original pain onto the significant people in their lives.

Lucy was excited when her best friend Carol invited her home to tea, but when she got there she was puzzled. There was no tense atmosphere around Carol's dad; Carol and her brother even seemed quite pleased to see him when he came home. They didn't cower when they heard his key in the lock like Lucy and her family did. But even more surprisingly, Carol's dad did not seem to look at Carol the same way Lucy's father looked at her. There was no subtle feeling of her breasts or sharp pressing of his body against hers, all disguised as a "hug". This was the first time Lucy realized that her family was not normal.

When a child suffers trauma outside the family, the family should provide the love, acceptance, and understanding that child needs in order to start healing. However, often families themselves are the source of the trauma or do not support the child when they are in pain, either because they are preoccupied with other problems or because they don't know how to.

Families: the ideal

Families are meant to be places where children are cherished as valuable people, and where a child's needs for nurture, unconditional love, and protection are met. The family is also the place where children can explore their personalities, and can learn about boundaries and inter-personal relationships. A home is ideally where children can become individuals in their own right and where they can freely express their thoughts and opinions.

It is important to remember that children do not think conceptually, but literally. They are not able to think, "Mum's having a bad day – she must be having her period. That's why she's being so grumpy!" Children believe what is said to them. So if a child is told, "You make me sick," or, "You're such a pain – you're so stupid," they believe that they've literally made the adult sick or that they are really stupid. Statements like this lodge in their hearts and become the foundation of how they see themselves as adults.

Although Yasmin is a qualified accountant and holds down a high-flying job in the city, she still suffers from extremely low self-esteem and feelings of intellectual inadequacy. In her family Yasmin was the "dim-wit", and everyone told her that at least twice a day. Meryl is a beautiful and successful model but is still very insecure about her looks. This is only understandable when you realize that her mother used to compare her to her sisters every day, saying, "Look at this girl – she is too tall and flat-chested. How is she ever going to get married?" Unsurprisingly, both these women struggle in their relationships today.

All families are imperfect

There is no perfect family. All families are tense or stressful in one way or another. However, some families are not just tense occasionally; they are abusive and dangerous for children. The deep human needs of the child are not met and the child therefore becomes damaged.

There is a popular saying which has a lot of truth in it:

> *"Sow a thought, reap an action. Sow an action, reap a habit.*
>
> *Sow a habit, reap a character. Sow a character, reap a destiny."*[1]

We can apply that saying to the way a child is treated when they are growing up. If the thoughts, actions, and habits we sow into a child's life are full of support, affirmation, and love, that child will grow up to be a confident, empowered adult who is able to engage in healthy relationships and make good choices in life. If the child receives the opposite, then that too will have consequences.

So what do children need from their families? Healthy families will display:

- Good communication – family members listen to each other and are listened to
- Resolution skills – conflicts and disagreements are not avoided but worked through

- Respect for each other – there is no shaming of individuals, and family members know they can talk freely about their needs and feelings
- Shared decision-making – everyone has a say and one person does not dominate
- Social accountability and support – there are outsiders who know the family and can give care and support when needed

This creates a safe place where there can be closeness and trust.

However, if a family does not meet these criteria in some or all areas, the children may find some parts of their adult lives very difficult – especially intimacy. Even worse, if they have a background of shame, rejection, and abuse, their inner selves will become distorted as they grow. The way they perceive life, others, reality, and self will all be coloured by this pain.

These families are termed "dysfunctional". But this does not mean the whole family experience is negative. When I look at my own family, I can see there were positive sides to it. My family was very creative and growing up in that atmosphere taught me a resourcefulness that has equipped me to problem-solve in a creative way. However, there were also very dysfunctional aspects to my family that were reflected in negative patterns of behaviour and ways of relating.

Family dysfunctions
The most common forms of family dysfunction could be said to be:

Denial
Families who are in denial can pretend that a situation which is obvious to everyone outside the home does not exist. This

is sometimes known as "the elephant in the room", meaning that if an outsider comes into the house, they can plainly see there is a situation (an elephant) in the room, but members of the family itself (sometimes all) refuse to admit it is there. An example of this is when a family has a member who drinks too much or takes drugs. This is the case with Joseph's father. It is obvious to Joseph's friends that Joseph's father is an alcoholic: he shakes, smells of drink, and has not held down a job for years. Yet Joseph's family refuse to admit there is a problem. Because of their refusal to confront the truth, the situation is perpetuated, and there is no hope of change.

Control and collusion
When one member of the family is very controlling, the rest of the family live in fear of their emotional outbursts and do not challenge them. In Jamila's family, her father was treated as a dictator who had to be obeyed no matter what his request. The six children did everything he wanted, because they knew that if they didn't he would rage and shout and use violence against them. In families like Jamila's, the rest of the family goes along with the person who is exerting this emotional pressure in order to avoid their anger. They can also collude with the situation by saying and doing nothing to challenge this.

No-go areas
Most families have verbal and non-verbal "no talk" rules. "No talk" rules can be healthy if, for example, the parents agree not to talk about their sex lives in front of the children. However, if no one is allowed to talk about sex at all, this becomes an unhealthy restriction. It is important to know who is implementing the "no talk" rule and what areas it covers.

Fuzzy boundaries

Some families have generational boundaries which are blurred, or there may be role confusion. For instance, a daughter may take a mother's role in a family. This might not just mean helping out in the kitchen, but perhaps having sole responsibility for caring for other children, or relating to her father more as a wife than a daughter. In this scenario, the adults become heavily reliant on the child instead of being there for the child. This could happen because of an illness or loneliness; but the result is that the child takes on the parenting role and the parent becomes very dependent on them emotionally.

In Andie's case, though, her father went further, and the relationship became not only emotionally dependent, but sexually incestuous too. Andie was fourteen when her mother became very ill and was hospitalized for many months. She cooked, cleaned, and prepared the dinner for her father every night. One evening she overheard her father saying to his friends, "She has become so much my wife I have begun to desire her as a woman." Her father never touched her physically, but understandably she found this comment extremely shocking and disturbing.

Social unaccountability

This is a problem that affects much of our society in the UK. Families today often live totally isolated lives and play no part in the community, as they may have done in the past, perhaps as part of a religious or social group. Neighbours may know the family superficially, but often do not know what is really happening inside the home. There is the added dilemma that if they do suspect something is wrong, they are unsure as to what action to take or who to talk to.

Repeating our unhappy past

All these dysfunctions form deep-seated impressions and can have a long-lasting effect on the child. This would not be so bad if it was just the childhood that was lost; but our childhood has a very profound effect on us later, whether for good or ill. At sixteen or eighteen we don't just leave behind our formative years and move on: in some strange way we keep repeating them for many years to come.

In their book *Love is a Choice*, psychologists Hemfelt, Minirth, and Meier describe this constant repetition of the past as "the Homing Instinct".[2] They claim that although we may leave home physically, within us there is an instinct to re-create our home of origin and familiar surroundings. Just as animals and birds migrate home to where they were reared, so humans seek to return "home" even if that home was not a happy place.

Home, however, is not an external geographic location but an internal place within our minds – something in us which seeks to reconstruct our childhood in our present lives. Daniella's father was extremely angry and dissatisfied with his marriage. As an adult, Daniella makes every effort to stay away from angry men. Yet despite their looks, nationalities, and circumstances being very different from her own background, Daniella keeps being drawn into relationships with angry men. Deep within her subconscious, Daniella is trying to "fix" her relationship with her dad. She transfers all her desires for her relationship with her father to work onto the men in her life, so that this time there can be a happy ending.

The most negative aspect of this homing instinct if our home has been dysfunctional is that these relationship patterns repeat themselves again and again, even if the actual people change. You carry on playing the same part, but surrounded by different people or situations. The only way out of this cycle for Daniella is for her to come to terms with her relationship with her father. She may well need support to do this, because it is unlikely that he will be able to help her.

It may help Daniella to recognize that:

- Her father was in a lot of pain when she was a child
- This was not her fault
- Her primary experience of men will be highly influenced by her father, as he was the main man in her life when she was a child
- Her relationship with him will never be what she needed as a child or even as an adult
- She needs to grieve the loss of the father relationship she deserved but never had
- With support she can work towards a place of acceptance

Having finally freed herself from this relationship, she will then be free to start choosing a different type of man to relate to. However, she will still need to:

- Recognize the type of men she is drawn to and look out for issues they may have with anger
- Stay accountable in her relationships and discuss what is going on in them

Playing a role

People who have been heavily enmeshed in their family problems and acted as the peacemaker often become "rescuers" in their adult lives. They are forever helping people – not in a healthy way but out of compulsion – and they may be internally very angry about it. This is true of isolated children, who often withdraw from life as an adult and live at a distance from those around them.

You can also see this pattern repeat down the generations. If your mother was a "hero"-type, the chances are her mother was too, and you could be tempted to play that role because it is what you have seen and know. People even choose careers in which they re-enact this role, although deep down they may be extremely unsatisfied and have the desire to do and be something different.

Let's look at some of the classic roles children may play in families and then go on to live out as adults.[3]

Family hero
As a child: Overly responsible, motivated by fear and guilt, can't say no, takes responsibility for other children or adults.
As an adult can become: A workaholic, manipulative, compulsive; can get into co-dependent relationships where they are the "carer" (see chapter seven).

Problem child/Scapegoat
As a child: Angry inside, troublemaker, seeks negative attention, withdrawn, defiant, hostile.
As an adult can become: A person who struggles with addiction, gets into trouble with the police, or possibly has unplanned pregnancies.

Lost child
As a child: Loner, daydreamer, distant, ignored, shy, drifter.
As an adult can become: Lonely or an outsider in groups, someone who doesn't voice feelings, has difficulties in communicating. Can seek to be lost in films, TV, and books.

Family clown
As a child: Immature, does anything for attention or a laugh, has a short attention span and difficulty concentrating at school.
As an adult can become: Compulsive clown, often on the verge of emotional outbursts, highly strung; someone who looks to be rescued in relationships.

· ·
NEW SHOES

Temi rushed into her support group, turning off her ringing phone, and apologized for being late again. As she relayed her day, which included a ten-hour shift at the nursery, picking up her friend's child from school, and cooking a meal for her ailing mother-in-law, the group felt exhausted just listening to her. When the subject turned to family roles, Temi began to see how her role in life was always to be the carer. Being the eldest child in a family with no dad and a mother who worked long shifts to support her children, Temi became the substitute mum for her siblings. On leaving school she got a job caring for children in a nursery, in which she excelled. She also helped her best friend to look after her daughter, and was expected by her husband to cook and clean for his disabled mother.

Temi began to see that in the career she had chosen and in the way she related to her friends and partner, she was repeating a role which began in her original family: the "family hero". Although painful, this was a breakthrough moment for Temi. She began to see that this was a role she did not want to play any more, if only because she was exhausted.

Role reversal

But how do you break out of a role which you have been playing for many years, possibly all your life?

First, you need to understand that your current behaviour is what is termed as "unfinished business". This refers to a situation (or business) from the past that is still having a subconscious hold over you today. Temi was acting out the role she played in her family in her current relationships and life choices. The way to get out of this cycle was for Temi to look at her childhood role, realize that she may still be playing it and why she might be doing that, and then look at ways of making some changes.

Secondly, a word of warning. Don't expect the people around you who know you in that role (especially if you are a "hero" type) to like it when you try to break out of the role! If you have been taking care of and rescuing others, the chances are they won't be delighted when you hand them back their responsibilities. Often, the hardest part of making a change is setting new boundaries with familiar people, and not giving in to those false feelings of guilt when you do.

Temi stopped doing unpaid overtime at work, put limits on the amount of free babysitting she was available for, and cut down on cooking for her mother-in-law. This was not without a lot of conflict and resistance both from inside herself and from those around her. However, with the help of her support group she was able to make some dramatic changes because she desired a different kind of life and wanted to explore other parts of her personality than the "caring" one. It was not an easy choice, but it was one Temi had to make in order to move forward.

Of course, Temi did continue to care, but gradually this became not out of compulsion from past pressures, but out of a desire to give and share that both she and the recipient found meaningful.

Leaving home

It is important to identify when you first started taking on the role you are playing, and what circumstances caused you to have to do this. Who were the people around you at that time and what were the needs that you felt you had to fulfil? Tracing your situation back to its root and seeing the difficulties you were experiencing then will help you to rebuild your personality. It will enable you to see that at that time you had no option, but today you can make an adult choice.

Take some time to think over the roles listed on page 86:

NEW SHOES

- Did you recognize any of the roles listed?
- Which role did you play?
- What about your brothers and sisters?
- Did your role change when you went to school?

Do you think you have continued that role today? Think about:
- Your choice of career or job
- Your hobbies and out-of-work activities
- How you relate to your partner
- What happens in your friendships

It is also important at these times of reassessment to seek help from friends whom you trust and who can support you in your new choices.

Mealtimes and families

If you are struggling to remember how your family related, it can be useful to think of a family mealtime in your house. Mealtimes reveal much about family relationships and often reflect what is going on in the family.

In some families, mealtimes are a place to share about the day, exchange ideas, and bond together. In other families the children eat separately from the parents. In some households mealtimes are when conflicts are aired. This can be positive if handled well or extremely negative if it is not.

For Celine, family mealtimes were full of apprehension. They were times when her parents would choose to express the frustrations of their relationship, either through a punishing silence or by shouting at each other. The children were extremely stressed and frightened during this time.

Those mealtimes exposed how tense and unhealthy Celine's home was. They left her and her siblings with problems in their close relationships and with very negative feelings towards any social event that involved food.

However, when Celine went to university she moved out of her family home and shared a house with people who all ate together. These were times of laughter, conversation, and connection. At first Celine sat away from the table on a nearby sofa, haunting memories of the family meals still fresh in her mind. But over the course of a year she began to feel safe enough to sit at the table with her friends, and meals became a positive experience that she enjoyed.

Think about your own family mealtimes:

- What was the atmosphere like around your family table?
- Did you all eat together or did some people eat separately?
- Were you all encouraged to discuss your day?
- Was it enjoyable or stressful?
- How do you feel about mealtimes now – do you enjoy them?
- What would make you feel safe about eating with others?

Put yourself in the picture
Draw a picture of your family.

- Where do you put yourself? Which room are you in?
- Who are you close to?
- Who did you want to be close to?

Draw a picture of yourself now with your current circle of friends or partner.

- Where would you be in that picture?
- Where would you like to be?
- What has to happen for you to get there?

Don't give up!

Leaving a role can be very uncomfortable – even if you don't like the way your life is being ruled by it. It is almost as though when you try to move away from the familiar, you feel lost and empty inside and wonder who you really are and what your life is now going to be founded on. It is hard work and it takes time and patience. But as your life gradually changes, new behaviour and thought patterns emerge.

Persistence is the key, and the fact that you are dissatisfied and desire healthier relationships is the crucial factor to moving towards that new life.

Remember that however small the changes you make are, the key is that you have started. In the words of a Chinese proverb, "The journey of a thousand miles begins with the first step."

Checkout sheet: Chapter five

1. How do you remember your family? How do you feel when you think of them?

2. Does it feel stressful to recall what it was like living in your childhood home?

3. Did you enjoy mealtimes as a child? If not, why not?

4. What do you need today in order to make mealtimes enjoyable?

5. Can you see what "unfinished business" you are trying to resolve today?

6. What would help you to move out of those familiar patterns?

CHAPTER SIX

RELATIONSHIPS: WHO'S GIVING, WHO'S TAKING?

Of the 13,237 children counselled for sexual abuse by ChildLine[1] in 2007–08 the vast majority were abused by someone they knew:

- 59 per cent said they had been sexually abused by a family member
- 29 per cent said they had been sexually abused by someone else known to them
- 4 per cent said they had been sexually abused by a stranger

These statistics reveal the extremely shocking reality that most victims of sexual abuse know or have a close relationship with their abuser. The victim is then left to deal with the very serious consequences of this betrayal and their powerlessness to stop it. It could be said that the closer the person is to the abuser, the more traumatic it will be for the victim and the more their future relationships will suffer damage.

The damage of powerlessness
Child sexual abuse is so horrific because it produces one of the most intense experiences of powerlessness. Most of the time, children are at the mercy of an adult world. They have very little power. Physically and intellectually, they have no way of gaining control of their situation. Who do they tell if

they are being violated? And perhaps more crucially, who will believe them? The pressure is even more intense if the abuser is a family member and the victim has to deal with the threat of being blamed for a family break-up. Sadly, the abuser is often a family member or someone close to the child.

Imagine a station or an airport. When a train or plane is unexpectedly cancelled, this usually produces a sense of frustration or even panic among the passengers. Why is this? It is because they are powerless to change their situation and they know it! They have no other way of getting to their destination, so they are in the hands of others. They have lost some personal control and power.

The results of powerlessness

The child who is sexually abused is often powerless on three levels. This is particularly true if the abuse occurs over a protracted time period and within a family situation:

• They cannot change their family or their circumstances

• They cannot stop the abuse

• They cannot end the personal pain

This sense of helplessness often leads to quite extreme responses in their adulthood relationships, such as being controlling, remaining a victim, or even giving up on relationships altogether through fear of betrayal and being powerless again.

Being controlling

The experience of powerlessness often leads to an extreme fear of being vulnerable or controlled, and can result in controlling behaviour patterns:

• Controlling relationships – never letting go in a
  relationship or revealing yourself

- Never allowing others (especially people you find attractive) to get close to you
- Always being the "carer" in relationships, never receiving support or love from others
- Trying to control other people through anger or manipulation
- Adopting controlling and obsessive rituals, such as keeping a home obsessively clean or tidy
- Being driven by compulsions, such as addiction to food, drugs, alcohol, fantasy, perfectionism, or even working all the time

Samantha seems doomed to live life in isolation, because no one is able to get close to her, and to be honest, no one really wants to. As a child she felt extremely powerless, being brought up in a family where she was not only the main carer for her disabled mother but was also abused by her father on a regular basis. Samantha had very little or no control over her life. This left her with an innate fear of being powerless in her adult life. After starting as a receptionist on her sixteenth birthday, Samantha has worked her way up – through hard work, evening classes, and hours of unpaid overtime – to become Head of Department in a large corporation. Unfortunately, she now has a problem with control. Although seemingly powerful, the slightest threat to her world – a difference of opinion, for example – will cause her tremendous inner trauma, and she then reasserts herself in a very aggressive way. She dismisses any suggestions or ideas that are not her own; and she actively demotes any person with potential, viewing them as a threat to the position she has had to work so hard to attain.

Like most controlling people, Samantha is not fun to be around. Of course, we can see that this all stems from deep-rooted inner pain, but who really cares about that when she is actively oppressing them? The sad fact is that controlling people are often the most hurting people in our community; but because they are so hard to get along with, they end up the most lonely and uncared for.

Remaining a victim

On the other hand, the sense of helplessness experienced in childhood can result in the victim not being able to take charge of life in an adult way, which then leads to re-victimization. Yvette's relationships with men are characterized by one over-riding factor: she gives, they take. When dating, she often finds she ends up picking up the tab at the restaurant or cinema. Once she even lent one of her boyfriends some money to buy her flowers. Pretty soon she finds she's financing not only her time with them, but their lifestyle – paying their rent, bills, or even credit cards. Then when she starts running out of money she finds the relationship starts to fade. Yvette keeps being re-victimized. She hasn't learned how to put up proper boundaries with men or even to spot men who are going to exploit her.

Other effects of helplessness include:

- Chaotic living: not being able to cope with everyday life or hold down a job or pay bills, etc.
- Not being able to take control in relationships or in life – finding yourself in situations or relationships you really don't want to be in
- Inability to make decisions – relying on others to do it for you
- Being re-victimized, for example, being abused in a relationship and accepting this as normal
- Remaining child-like in your relationships

- Being unable to trust your own instincts, which could leave you open to re-abuse
- Repeating damaging relationships, and not being able to see you are repeating the pattern
- Being attracted to people who are controlling

Sadly, it is quite common to find that abuse is not a one-off occurrence. Some people who are victimized as children go on to become re-victimized as adults through their sexual relationships or friendships, at work, or even sometimes with strangers who sense they are vulnerable.

The lack of boundaries the victim experienced as a child means that they are unable to set appropriate boundaries with those around them when they mature. They can perceive as "normal", behaviour which others might see to be totally unacceptable. Sandy, for example, did not recognize that her boyfriend's behaviour was extremely abusive. It took her friend Julia to point out to her that being called names and treated as a possession was totally unacceptable. Having grown up in a family with an extremely controlling father, to Sandy this was just the regular pattern of how men treated women.

Being emotionally dead

There is also another side-effect to being continuously in a place of powerlessness. Eventually, you become numb to it and it doesn't affect you any more. This feeling of internal deadness is rooted in trauma or abuse that the child is unable to prevent. Unable to express the feelings within, they forfeit the pain through:

- Denial and memory loss: pretending it isn't happening or never happened
- Splitting off: retreating into fantasy or dissociating mentally from the situation

- Emotional emptiness: becoming numb and simply not feeling anything any more

These all lead to a gradual deadening inside – a sense of giving up on life and people. This dead feeling carries on into adulthood, bringing with it a sense of numbness or withdrawal from life and what it has to offer.

Feeling hopeful or emotional seems dangerous to Chris, who works quietly at her desk all day saying little to those around her, and then spends the evenings alone watching TV. Her weekends are spent sleeping for most of the day and she has little contact with the outside world, aside from making frequent visits to watch movies so she can escape from her own loneliness. Chris is emotionally dead inside. Those around her often don't notice or include her – it is almost as though she has disappeared from life.

Chris was abused as a child and the powerlessness she felt resulted in her eventually closing down her feelings to protect herself. To some extent, she is still perpetuating that feeling today. However, with some help Chris could make another choice. She could choose to want to be emotionally alive, even if that feels frightening. It is only after this decision has been made that she will be able to think through what she wants from her life and how she needs to be re-empowered to attain it.

Regaining power and establishing boundaries

One critical way of regaining a healthy sense of power is by looking at your boundaries.

Boundaries are there to let the good in and keep the bad out. In our world, we all live within certain boundaries. You can't, for instance, just walk into a stranger's house and start trying on their clothes and eating the food from their fridge – not without being arrested anyway! This is because that person's door is the boundary to their house. It says, "You can go so far but no further without my permission."

Powerlessness leads to victims being unable to set appropriate boundaries in their lives, as in Sandy and Yvette's situations. Most small children have no boundaries, no internal way to protect themselves from abuse. So the powerlessness and lack of dignity a child is subjected to will influence the boundaries they are able to set later on.

If boundaries were not established clearly in a person's childhood, as an adult their boundaries will usually be impaired. They will overcompensate either by being too over-protective, and therefore entering into controlling and manipulative behaviour; or by not being protective enough and unable to take any control over their lives, leaving them vulnerable to further abuse.

Where there has been abuse and the child is left powerless, the adult victim often gives away power to others in a similar way, or tries to take control of other people's boundaries in the same way that theirs were violated. Neither is a healthy response.

It is useful to look at good and bad boundaries so that we can recognize them and perhaps improve on them when it is beneficial to do so.

Good boundaries

Good boundaries are not walls; they are permeable, and let the good in and keep the bad out. True boundaries are never selfish. They give us space to regroup and gain strength to love people. Good boundaries give us a sense of ourselves and who we really are.

In addition, boundaries affect the way we gain energy and strength. This will also be partly due to our personality type:

• Extroverts regroup and gain strength from other people

• Introverts regroup and gain strength on their own

Both types are equally valid. Which do you think you are?

Bad boundaries
Bad boundaries come in different forms:

People who can't say "no"
These people cannot say "no" to another person because they fear that setting a boundary and expressing their desires will cause conflict or loss of relationship with the other person.

People who can't hear "no"
These people cannot take responsibility for their own lives and often manipulate others into doing what they want by not responding to legitimate limits set by others.

People who can't say "yes"
These people are often walled off from connecting to others. Even when people reach out to them in a healthy way, they do not engage. They remain internally in control, but isolated and lonely.

People who can't hear "yes"
These people do not respond to the genuine and healthy needs of those around them for support and relationship, often acting in a dismissive way and avoiding closeness.[2]

Often we can exhibit a combination of all of these and react differently in various situations. For example, at work we may have no problem setting boundaries, but with a partner it can be very different – or vice versa.

Rebuilding the boundaries in relationships
Good boundaries mean you can be intimate with others and yet not lose a sense of yourself. You can be attached

but separate – a person in your own right. In relationships with bad boundaries you may give up feelings, ideas, and opinions; but in emotionally healthy relationships you can be close to someone and yet disagree without any harm being done to the relationship.

In some ways boundaries can be the ultimate test of a relationship. If you can't say "no" and "I don't agree" without harming the relationship then something needs to change.

However, learning to change boundaries is a tricky task as they may have been embedded for years. The first step is trying to recognize where your boundaries are.

Check out your boundaries

Take a look at the questions below and see if any of these have applied to you in recent weeks.

- Do you have difficulty saying "no"?
- Are there some people you always give in to?
- When you are out with friends or a partner, who makes the choices about where you go and what you do?
- What happens if you don't agree with your parents; your partner; your best friend?

If you don't agree with them, what are the consequences for you? Do they make your life difficult or do they respect your space? Sometimes it is healthy to be persuaded to another point of view, but if this is always the case and you come under a lot of pressure, then you may need to do some work on strengthening your boundaries.

- Which people do you find it most difficult to put up boundaries with?
- How could you put up better boundaries with them?
- Are there people in your life who love your "no" as well as your "yes"?

. . . .

Do you feel victimized at times but are not sure if you are right? Check this out with someone you trust who will give you an honest answer. Try to assess your relationships:

- Do people respect your opinion and count it as valid? Or do you often find yourself having to back down to others?
- Do you find it hard to hear someone else's opinion on something you feel strongly about?
- Does that threaten you?
- How much do you think you really listen to other people and their feelings?
- Do you think you receive support more than you give it?

People who have damaged boundaries need to learn new ways of relating and behaving. It is healthy and progressive to realize that we have rights in relationships with others, and that others also have rights in their relationship with us.

Betrayal by someone close to you

Deception is the worst thing that can happen in a relationship. Everyone has a story about how they have been betrayed. But when a child is betrayed, this has huge implications for the relationships that child will have as an adult.

Sexual abuse, and particularly incest, is often betrayal by a person you are intimate with. The more intimate the relationship, the deeper the betrayal, and the more difficult it is going to be for the child to form deep and trusting relationships with others in adult life. This is especially true if the abuser is one of the few people in the child's life who has made them feel "special". This relationship may have been formed over many years, so the betrayal for the child is even more traumatic.

Some children are the victims of abusers who come from outside into that child's life specifically to abuse them. This is known as "grooming". The child is set up by the abuser, who may manipulate and seduce the child with gifts and affection. This may be the first time the child has received such attention, and they may crave and enjoy it, which makes the deception even greater.

Not just one betrayal

There is also a further betrayal that causes much pain: betrayal by the people who could have helped but chose not to.

Every child is a member of some kind of community – their school, their neighbourhood. But often people choose not to intervene in a child's life when they suspect abuse, some through ignorance, some through denial, and others through fear. Of course, this leaves the child in an abusive situation for much longer.

This non-intervention can take the form of[3]:

• Collusion: they directly encourage the abuse
• Denial: they ignore all the evidence and pretend it isn't happening
• Self-protection: they don't challenge the abuser because they fear for their own personal safety and mental welfare

The child is then left alone, feeling guilty and confused, and often blaming themselves. This is frequently because being betrayed by someone they were close to is so unbearable that self-blame or denial seems like a preferable option.

Relationships and betrayal

Relationships become very difficult when we have been betrayed, so we may become isolated and avoid them.

When we enter a friendship or a relationship, as soon as we experience losing some personal control it can put us straight back in touch with the pain we felt when we were abused.

We may feel we don't want to risk another disappointment, so we become distrusting of people. We may even subconsciously sabotage our relationships to avoid the closeness they bring. Without the risk of closeness and trust, the fear of betrayal is controlled. But we can end up killing our desire for relationship with others, leaving ourselves extremely isolated.

The damage of betrayal plays itself out in relationships in several ways:

Fear of intimacy
- Core trust has been lost, so we have huge difficulties in trusting people again
- Being close to someone becomes very frightening

Suspicion[4]
- We are suspicious of people's motives for being close to us
- We wait for someone to let us down or betray us
- We anticipate being let down so let others down first in order to keep control

Sexualization and confusion in relationships
- We avoid intimate relationships because sex is associated with betrayal, so any relationship that has the potential to become physically close is dangerous
- We confuse closeness with sexuality

Denial
- We latch onto partial truths that our minds tell us

- We avoid betrayal by living in fantasy and half-truths
- We are unaware of what is obvious to others, avoiding the truth

Being over-analytical
- We have an over-awareness of what people think about us
- We are constantly concerned about others
- We lack objectivity, reading too much into situations
- We over-analyse situations
- We are constantly looking for others to betray us

These behaviour patterns lead to us becoming increasingly suspicious of others and finding it extremely hard to trust.

Being suspicious

People who have been betrayed are often extremely apprehensive about intimate relationships to the degree that they can become very cynical about those around them. This clearly makes relationships stressful both for the person and for their friends, partner, and family. Mistrustful people live their lives on guard at all times; their cynicism pervades everything they do, say, and believe about themselves and others. They are highly sceptical of other people and their motives for wanting to be in a relationship with them.

Suspicion takes a current situation and gives it an extremely negative spin. It takes us down a road of worry and anxiety, creating scenario after scenario of ever-worsening outcomes. It is like having an internal "spin doctor", but the spin is all negative. This can result in feelings of paranoia around others. Each slight change in voice tone is noted and analysed; a text can be read and re-read countless times; an email will be written and re-written endlessly. It is almost like playing a waiting game: predicting (often inaccurately) that the betrayal is coming and watching for clues, in order to prepare for it.

Other people who have been betrayed, however, are not prepared to sit and wait to be betrayed again, so they seize control of the situation and end the relationship. This provides the illusion of being in control. But the tragedy is that potentially healthy relationships are ended needlessly. This is true in Martin's relationship. Latching on to half-truths and scrutinizing his girlfriend's every text and email, Martin prepared to confront her. Interrogating her over a comment on her Facebook page, he pushed her into a corner and she reacted angrily out of hurt and astonishment. Full of mistrust, Martin believed his girlfriend was going to leave him, and in some ways he manipulated the situation so that she did.

Rebuilding trust

How then do you overcome the trauma of past betrayal? How can you drop your suspicions and begin to rebuild trust?

Recognize you're being suspicious

First, as with all unhealthy behaviours, the initial step is to recognize that you are doing it. Catch yourself when you sense yourself spiralling down into your own distrusting thought patterns. Even more illuminating is to count how many times a day or a week you find yourself having these thoughts.

Slow down

Secondly, try to be "in the moment" for a few minutes. You could do this by focusing on breathing in and out slowly, or by rooting your feet firmly on the ground. This will give your mind a couple of minutes to calm itself.

Write it down
Thirdly, record all your negative thoughts on a notepad, diary, or iphone. Over time you will notice when you are most likely to spiral into these thoughts. Thinking back, do these times remind you of anything from your past? You may need help to do this: perhaps talk it through with a counsellor or support group.

Replace the negative thoughts
Try to get into the habit of talking positively to yourself. Instead of thinking, "My partner is late again… it's the third time this week. Perhaps he is losing interest in me. I wonder if he's having an affair? Why was he checking his phone last night? This relationship is almost certainly over!" perhaps you could try something along the lines of, "My partner is late again… it's the third time this week and I'm finding this difficult. We need to sit down together and work out a good communication plan for when he's going to be late so I can still relax and enjoy my evening."

The plus side!
Is it feasible that there are any positive sides to being a "suspicious" person? Well, I think there could be. A person who struggles with mistrust and suspicion is also often extremely sensitive and therefore able to pick up easily on other people's feelings.

There are of course negative sides to this too, but what a perceptive and responsive person to have as your ally! In this world where there is so much loneliness and so many people's suffering goes unnoticed, what a fantastic friend or partner to have!

Learning to trust

We need to be wise; not everyone is trustworthy. We need to accept this without being suspicious of everyone. There are certain attributes we can observe in people that give us clues as to whether we should take the risk of entering a deeper relationship with them.

What are some of the attributes that would indicate to you that a person is trustworthy? Here are some ideas to contemplate:

- Arriving on time
- Listening to you
- Sharing areas of their lives
- Taking it in turns to choose how to spend your time together
- Keeping commitments and promises
- Being open to your point of view when problems and issues arise
- Being willing to look at themselves and make changes
- Respecting your personal values

Obviously being in close relationships means that we will experience difficulties at times as issues arise. This is not negative in itself; the important point is that you are able to talk these problems through and find an outcome you are both happy with.

You can't confront every single little issue, but if it concerns respect, equality, or your values, you need to address it.[5] You can do this by stating:

- What you are finding difficult/hurtful
- How it makes you feel and act
- What you would like changed
- What will happen if there is no change

For example, if a partner you have been dating for six months is extremely critical of you and sometimes calls you names, you need to:

- State that it is hurtful and disrespectful to be treated in this way
- Explain that it makes you feel angry and hurt and distances you from them
- Say you would like them to stop doing this and to talk respectfully about your differences
- Let them know that if there is no change in the behaviour, you will be re-assessing whether you want to continue dating them, or limiting the time you spend with them

Once you have done this you need to:

- Take note of how the other person responds
- See if they are willing to own their part in what happened
- Critically, find out if they are open to change

If they dismiss it, deny it, or become very defensive, you may need to think about how deeply you want to be involved with this person. If you are in a permanent relationship, you should consider getting some support to deal with these issues.

Learning to trust is a long and painful road. Start with small steps. Consider going for a coffee with a friend and revealing something about yourself that you may not have told them before. This will bring confidence that leads on to more major changes in your relationship. We may not always get it right, but having an open attitude to other people gives us the opportunity to break out of isolating behaviours and grow to be better friends and partners.

Checkout sheet: Chapter six

1. Can you think of any ways in which you seek to control your life or relationships?

2. Did your family have good boundaries?

3. Were you allowed boundaries as a child?

4. Has this affected your boundaries with people as an adult?

5. Which people do you find it hardest to put up boundaries with?

6. How could you put up better boundaries?

7. Are there people in your life who love your "no" as well as your "yes"?

CHAPTER SEVEN

CO-DEPENDENCY: CAN'T LIVE WITHOUT YOU

When Sylvie came over from Malaysia to train as a doctor in London, she was very grateful that Denise, who was also on her course, took a special interest in her. Helping her to settle into a new life, not to mention a new nation, Denise spent many hours with Sylvie in her first few months at college. After a while Sylvie began to want to make new friends and spend time with other students. But Denise became very angry and her behaviour changed dramatically.

Sylvie recalls:

> At first I was happy she took such an interest in me – she seemed really caring, and as I was new to England it was nice to feel so special and wanted. But then I felt she began 'mothering' me in a way that I didn't want. I'd already left home and I didn't want another mother. I tried to pull away from her but she didn't seem to take the hint – in fact, it made her worse. She started telling me what to do even more, ringing me constantly, asking me where I was going out and what I was doing, even who I was talking to in college.
>
> In the end I gave in and carried on the relationship, but I found it suffocating and so stopped returning her calls. She said I was ungrateful, that I had only passed the first year exams with her help, and that without her I would fail the second year. She made me feel very guilty.

It's almost as though she likes to feel superior to me in some ways and feels that as long as I need her, she can boss me around. I've already had one controlling parent in my life (my mum) and I don't need another one.

I know I have lots of problems to work through, but I think in many ways she has more. The difference is: I know what my issues are. She doesn't seem to recognize hers and wants to run away from them by 'helping' other people.

Sylvie is right. Denise has a problem with controlling others and being co-dependent in relationships. It is my observation that many people who have been sexually abused come from families or environments that are unhealthy, and they often end up in relationships that are co-dependent. This is because they are basing their idea of what a relationship should be on what was modelled to them by their own family as they were growing up. It can also be true that the experience of being abused is one of being controlled, so victims of abuse can be drawn into relationships which they control or which are controlled in a way that could be termed co-dependent.

What is co-dependency?
You will probably have heard of the term "co-dependency". It is a word that has become part of our language and usually refers to relationships that are not considered healthy.

The term "co-dependency" originates from the Alcoholics Anonymous movement, which was set up to help the families of the alcoholic or the "dependent". They found that although it was the alcoholic who appeared to have the problem, the families or co-dependents of the addict also needed help. In many cases, the very fact that they had found themselves in a relationship with an addict indicated that they themselves had problems which needed to be dealt with. They observed

NEW SHOES

that they often "rescued" the addict, and in so doing, their intervention effectively helped the addict to stay addicted.

When Jane's husband Bob went on a drinking binge, it was Jane who rang up his boss the next morning and said he couldn't come in due to a sore throat, when he really had a hangover. It was Jane who paid off the credit card bill which he had run up at the bar. In fact, it was Jane who reaped the consequences of Bob's behaviour – by keeping Bob from having to take responsibility for his own actions.

But it is not only people involved with those who have addictions who struggle with co-dependency. Co-dependency is defined by Hemfelt, Minirth, and Meier in their book *Love is a Choice* as "an addiction to people, behaviour, or things".[1] A co-dependent person is one who tries to control their inner feelings by using people, or things outside themselves. The issue of control is very important.

Characteristics of a co-dependent person

A co-dependent person is often driven by the problems of their childhood family – whether they are aware of this or not. This can mean the person:

- Struggles with addictive and compulsive behaviour patterns, such as drinking or working all the time
- Has relationships that are not healthily separate, in which they or the other person become very dependent. Alternatively, they could be very isolated and distant
- Feels overly responsible for other people – looks after another person as though they were a child
- Tries to change things that they need to accept – finds it difficult to acknowledge that sometimes situations or people will not change
- Does not have a balanced lifestyle and may exhibit extreme behaviour patterns

• •

The roots of co-dependency

Co-dependency is rooted in a person's family origins. When a family becomes dysfunctional (see chapter five), a child's false self emerges and their true self becomes buried. As a result, they become submerged in a role of trying to keep the peace, or looking after one of their parents, or perhaps cooking and cleaning for the rest of the family.

Co-dependents become used to fixing, caring for, and looking after others, to make sure nothing really bad happens within the family. In Fran's home everyone worked really hard to make sure Dad never lost his temper, because when he did it would result in a frightening torrent of rage. Every evening Fran checked that the TV was switched on to her dad's favourite programme when he walked in, and that the lounge looked just as he liked it, quickly putting away any of her toys. This became the pattern for her adult life. Just like Temi, in chapter five, Fran became involved in relationships where she had to do the caring, often expecting nothing for herself.

Most of the relationships in Fran's life had elements of co-dependency. But there is also another type of dependency, which is known as emotional enmeshment. This is when a person forms an unhealthy attachment to one particular person at a time.

Emotional enmeshment

Emotional enmeshment often develops out of well-intentioned friendships which become too intense and clingy because of the neediness of the people involved. Instead of the other person being part of your life, they become the centre of your life. When this happens, an unhealthy attachment forms and the relationship becomes suffocating.

Emotionally enmeshing relationships are characterized by obsession. They tend to be very possessive, with an inclination towards excluding others. This can be taken to the extreme of subverting the other person's relationships so that there are no "outsiders". These partnerships are often also extremely tactile, to the extent that physical affection is displayed in a way that makes others feel uncomfortable.

The glue, if you like, which holds these relationships together is manipulation. One or perhaps both people seek to control the other person so that their other friendships, or career, or outside interests are all sabotaged in case they become a threat to the relationship.

Co-dependent and enmeshing relationships become intense very quickly – possibly marriage or permanent partnership is discussed straight away. Imagine that starting new friendships is like dealing out a pack of cards: one card should be given away to one person at a time. In an emotionally dependent relationship, however, the whole deck is given away to one person at once!

The roles which people play within these relationships can also become confused. For example, one partner almost becomes "the child", while the other person becomes "the parent". The person who once did the caring in their original family often adopts the role of parent, being attracted to and attracting friends who are childlike or partners they can look after, as they did at home. Needless to say, this is very unhealthy for both people.

Another characteristic of a co-dependent relationship is that one partner will exhibit an intense need to be needed.

Needing to be needed

Our communities would be cold and lonely places if people didn't support each other. However, there are some people who appear to "overcare" for others. It is not so much that what they are doing is wrong, but their motives may not be as clear cut as they appear on the surface. Although they may not be conscious of it, looking after others is actually a way of avoiding themselves. Inside they may be saying, "Let me fix your pain so I don't have to deal with my own." This is another form of co-dependency, a deep need to be looked up to – to almost "parent" another adult instead of being their equal.

This kind of co-dependency can often be found among the caring professions – for example, social workers, nurses, care-workers – although of course this is not true of all people in these jobs. It is also evident in other communities or organizations. In a church situation, for example, you tend to find that the same people do all the volunteering and their name is on every rota.

A healthy responsibility
A good example of a healthy way to care for another person can be seen in the famous parable of the Good Samaritan. This story shows how the Good Samaritan cared for the man who was beaten up and left for dead at the side of the road. He took the man to a local inn (or hotel as it would be today) and paid the manager to take care of him for a few days. The parable does not say the Samaritan paid for him to be looked after for the next fifteen years! He helped the man to get back on his feet and then trusted him to look after himself.

The problem with overcaring is that it not only leaves the "carer" feeling exhausted and eventually angry, it also disempowers the person they are helping and prevents them from taking up their full role as an adult. This is obviously not good for either person.

Detached relationships
Conversely, some people have relationships that are just as damaging because they keep themselves at a distance emotionally from those around them. They may even be

married or living together, but they still do not actually engage with the other person – there is no real intimacy. They are living "parallel lives" instead of lives that are connected. Problems are avoided and conflicts are not resolved. Alex, for example, has changed her job twice and not even told her husband. She lives her own life and does not share it with him. She is also unaware that her partner is nearing bankruptcy. With such little communication between them, there is no place for sharing problems and getting support. These people have learned that to share is too dangerous, so they prefer to keep their lives separate from others.

Co-dependency, emotional dependency, and detachment are all relational problems and therefore they need relational solutions. However, before we launch into new relationships, it can be extremely useful to understand our past. By looking back we can begin to recognize patterns in the relationships that are most important to us, so that we can move forward and make better choices for the future.

Make a love list

Make a list of the significant people in your life.[2] Write down their names and their relationship to you: for example, "Greg – Husband; Larry – Boss". This is a useful way of finding out what kind of people you are drawn to. This may sound strange, but it is actually a very useful tool for finding patterns or themes that run through your relationships, and it can be extremely illuminating.

When compiling your list:

• Don't judge yourself
• Include people you may have had only short relationships with
• Don't forget your close friends and flatmates

Can you think of words to describe them? For example:

- Considerate
- Committed
- Creative
- Broke
- Demanding
- Moody
- Intense
- Shy
- Angry
- Sexually attractive
- Detached
- Withdrawn

Here are some further questions to think about:

- What was it about them you were initially drawn to?
- What was their job – if they were in work?
- Did you spend more time listening to them or did they mostly listen to you?
- Can you see any of your family traits in any of these people?
- Who made most of the decisions in the relationship?
- Did you ever lend them money? Did you borrow money from them?
- Were you hurt by them? If so how?
- How did the relationship end – if it has ended?
- When you think of the relationship, what sort of feelings does it immediately arouse in you – a smile, a shudder, feelings of warmth?

Once you have written your lists, see if you can find any themes between people that keep re-occurring. Can you link any of these patterns back to your original family?

Understanding that we are drawn to certain types of people gives us the insight we need in order to make different choices or run our relationships differently in the future.

We cannot find healing if we remain alone. We need to form healthy relationships with appropriate levels of attachment and separateness so that we can share our needs and connect with people, and yet retain all our own goals, opinions, and personality. Our goal in relationships should be to be interdependent – to experience both closeness and independence, which leads to healthy intimacy.

So what is a healthy relationship?

Healthy relationships

Love is a choice! You can't make someone love you or want to be your friend. But as we work on ourselves and become more emotionally healthy, we will in turn attract healthier people.

Here are some examples of what a healthy relationship might look like:

Sacrificial
A healthy relationship will put the other person first, even if there is a cost involved. For instance, if your best friend gets a career opportunity or a place at a college in another city, you will acknowledge the loss but let them go freely, even though it means you may not see them as much as you would like.

Releasing
Being in a healthy relationship means wanting the other person to be all they can be – not wanting to restrict them or hold them back.

Inclusive, not exclusive

One person cannot fulfil every need you have! A healthy relationship will encourage other friendships and outside interests, not cling desperately to it as though it is the only thing that makes life bearable.

Able to acknowledge difference

In healthy relationships, people feel free to express their opinions, even if that means they do not always agree. The relationship is strong enough to take the challenge of a difference of opinion.

Mutually sharing

In a healthy relationship, both people recognize their need for support and in turn recognize the need to give support to the other person. They face life as a team, rather than as individuals who rely solely on themselves.

Time is your friend

When we first meet someone new it can be extremely exciting! Some research suggests that when we are in the first heady romantic days, there are actual physical changes taking place in our bodies. The brain releases more endorphins, which make us feel good and enhance our sense of security and comfort, so we feel physically and emotionally positive about ourselves. We can become absorbed in the other person's world and it can be tempting to put the rest of our lives on hold in order to focus on this relationship. Of course we have to make room for this new person, but we need to take time to do this. It is crucial that we stay close to our friends in the early stages of the relationship and don't allow ourselves to be swept out of our support systems so that one person becomes the centre of our whole life.

It is inappropriate in the first few weeks of meeting someone to tell them all your problems, or to expect them to be there for you in the middle of the night, or to lend you money. It is also inappropriate to start talking about marriage or moving in on the first date. You are both building a relationship together, and that takes time. .

The stages of a relationship
Healthy relationships are constructed in stages. These stages may develop as follows.

A new friendship
Although the beginning of a relationship is very exciting, you need to spend time getting to know that person. At this stage it is good to:

- Be interested in them. Ask them questions about themselves, listen carefully to their answers, and respond to them. Be positive about what they share!

- Learn about their hopes and dreams. Find out where they want to go in life and what plans they might have for the future.

- Be honest about yourself. Don't try to pretend to be something you are not. If they like heavy metal music and you don't, don't try to bluff it by telling them you love Slipknot or Metallica – they will soon find out you've faked it!

- Be trustworthy. Do what you say and stick to arrangements, even if something better comes along.

- Keep good boundaries. Meeting a new friend or possible partner can be thrilling, but don't be tempted to give away too much of yourself in the early phase.

A closer friendship

Once a solid friendship has been established, you may want to get to know the other person at a deeper level. This could mean you are able to:

- Be there for encouragement and support (when they need it). Learn what is going on in their life and support them when they need it – for example, before a job interview or a difficult meeting with their boss.

- Look for support yourself. Be vulnerable – let the other person know if you are feeling anxious or stressed. Sometimes we don't get support because we don't ask for it.

- Notice if you are doing all the giving or all the taking. This is important. If you are doing all the listening or all the paying, or vice versa, then it is time to take stock of the relationship and re-establish a balance. It is easy to lose healthy boundaries when you feel passionate about someone.

- Get to know in more detail what they want out of life. If you are planning a long-term relationship with someone, you need to find out what they want to do with their life. For example, if they plan to move abroad in the next year you need to consider if this fits in with your plans.

An intimate relationship

Some relationships, such as with your partner or spouse, can grow to be much more intimate. In these relationships it is important and appropriate that both people are:

- There to give comfort in trials. You can rely on one another to stand by and give special support through difficulties and heartaches, such as redundancy or caring for a sick parent.

- Committed to being loyal (within set boundaries). If the relationship begins to have a sense of permanence, you may wish to openly state that the relationship is now exclusive and that you consider each other in your plans for the future.

- Sensitive to the traits that the other person may need to work through. As the relationship progresses, you will become aware of weaknesses and problems in the other person. You need to think through whether these are weaknesses you can live with. Some issues are more serious than others. For example, struggling with addiction is different to being messy. Serious issues need to be addressed before the relationship becomes permanent.

- Aware of the areas in themselves that need working on. As with your partners or close friends, you may also have issues that need to be addressed. For serious problems such as addiction to drugs or alcohol you need to seek support and accountability. No matter how much you are drawn to another person, it is important that you face yourself first. Any problems you have outside a relationship will only be magnified inside it.

- Not trying to change the other person. Although change can often be very positive, if your new friend or partner is putting a lot of pressure on you to compromise on your beliefs or values – for example, changing your religion, dress sense, or your purpose in life – you need to take some space to think through if that is right for you. It is also good to talk to other friends and seek their advice.

Time is one element you cannot cheat in a relationship. But often in our insecurity we may wish to rush ahead to the next stage when we haven't really built a strong enough foundation in the initial stages. This can leave the other person feeling overwhelmed and could lay the groundwork for a co-dependent relationship.

When you are considering dating, one good way to ensure your relationship maintains healthy boundaries is to keep in touch with your friends throughout the dating process.

Listen to your friends

Don't even attempt to start dating when you have no friends around you – for example, if you have just moved to a new town or started at college. Don't date when your support system is 100 miles away. Always date when you are settled into a community and have established your own personal life and made your own contacts.

If you have recently started dating, here are some points you may need to be aware of:

- If you don't introduce your date to your friends, ask yourself why

- Be open to everything your friends have to say, even if you don't like hearing it

- Don't be swept out of your own life, hobbies, and interests by your new date

In our choice of friends or partners, we need to cultivate relationships with people who will support us and love our "no" as much as they love our "yes". We need to be able to receive care as well as give it.

We may also need to learn to love and enjoy our own company. Having some time on our own gives us the opportunity to reflect on our options and decide what we want out of life and relationships in the future.

Checkout sheet: Chapter seven

• •

1. Did you write down a love list? Did you manage to see a pattern?

2. Are you drawn to a certain type of person?

3. Do you think you do some things out of a need to be needed?

4. Do you think you could be avoiding some issues by caring for others?

5. Can you think of some relationships you have which are healthy?

6. What are the elements that make them a positive impact on your life?

CHAPTER EIGHT

SEXUAL AMBIVALENCE: YOU'RE HOT AND COLD

Eva has no problem attracting men. She says herself she can walk into a club and have any man she wants. Men will be drawn to her, and she allows them to get close to her to a certain degree. This could be a twenty-minute chat over a few drinks, or even a relationship that will last a few weeks. However, a relationship with Eva never lasts longer than that and it is always Eva who finishes it. Eva experienced sexual abuse as a child and is now extremely confused about relationships – especially sex.

We live in a society that seems obsessed with sex. Sex is used in the West to sell almost everything: TV, films, music, cars, even seemingly mundane products like bread or biscuits. Some aspects of the media in particular can imply that you aren't really a complete person unless you are having lots of sex. If, however, you have experienced sexual abuse as a child, you will have seen a different side of sex. Instead of something positive and life-enhancing, you may view sex as something difficult or even disgusting.

What sex should be

Sex is supposed to be about a shared experience – a source of comfort and strength for two people who are deeply involved with each other. John Gray, a relationships counsellor and the author of *Men are from Mars and Women are from Venus*, describes sex between a couple as a reminder of "the tender and highest love that originally drew them together. The alchemy of great sex generates the chemicals in the brain and body that allow the fullest enjoyment of one's partner. It increases our attraction to each other, stimulates greater energy, and even promotes better health."[1] Sex symbolizes one of the key aspects of a relationship: that it is about giving and receiving.

It is worth looking at where our feelings about sex originated from so that we can understand how they influence us today. Think for a moment about how you feel about your sexuality, and how those feelings developed when you were a child, a teenager, and a young adult. Here are some questions that might help you to think about this:

- What kind of sex education did you have?
- Did it equip you to make good life choices?
- Was there a trusted adult you could talk to if you needed more help: As a child? As a teenager?
- Was sex openly discussed in your family or was it a taboo topic?
- Was sex discussed too much? Did it feel intrusive or inappropriate?
- What was your family's attitude towards nudity and bodily functions?
- What kind of discussions about sex took place in the playground?
- Were your friends understanding about your views or did they make you feel left out?

Whether you are having sex or not, your sexuality is still a fundamental part of you: it is at the very core of your being. This is why, if it is violated, the effects are so devastating.

• •

Sex can be confusing

It is not hard to see why it is so difficult to feel in touch with your sexuality now if you were abused as a child. Sex may be something you want to avoid at all costs, because it brings up feelings of fear and confusion.

If you have been sexually abused, you may not want to face the fact that your body can respond to touch. Although this is understandable, recognizing why this happens is the way out of the false guilt you may be carrying. Our bodies are created to respond to sexual stimulation, and you may have felt pleasure during abuse or even experienced orgasm. This is not unusual. It also does not negate the fact that you were violated and that your consent was cruelly taken from you. An abuse happened, and as we saw in chapter two, it was rooted in the initial intentions of the abuser; you were innocent.

However, natural body responses can be a source of great remorse and confusion for victims of sexual abuse. Some victims can begin to believe that, because their body responded, they were somehow responsible for the abuse, or even colluded in it. A manipulative abuser who notices body responses may even use this as evidence that the victim "enjoyed it" and there was no coercion involved. You can see how easily this could happen to a young man or boy if he experiences an erection while being abused. Although the idea that he colluded in it is clearly untrue, it can lead to a chronic sense of false responsibility in the victim, since the very thing that he so despised brought him some degree of pleasure.

This can then lead to deep-rooted feelings of ambivalence towards sex and sexuality.

Why it's hard to feel sexy now

Ambivalence can be defined as the co-existence of two conflicting desires. A person can experience two contradictory emotions at the same time – for instance, joy and sorrow, happiness and sadness. This bewildering cross-current of emotions is most likely to be tapped into by a victim of abuse at moments of sexual awareness, when the enjoyment of the moment is confused with the pain of the past. This could be when you feel an attraction to another person or while you are making love to your partner.

Sexual ambivalence is especially prevalent if the abuser was known intimately to the victim; for example, if they were a relation. If you were fond of that person and had a seemingly positive relationship with them, the fact that this person went on to violate you justifiably leaves your mind in chaos. It is also true that if you experienced very little love or affection during your childhood, and were then offered some attention which turned abusive, you will feel extremely confused or even guilty. Something you legitimately needed turned into something horrific. It is a bit like biting into an apple and realizing half way through that you have eaten a maggot.

Sexual desire can then become connected in your mind to feelings of betrayal and powerlessness. This can continue into your adult relationships, where legitimate sexual pleasure or even just a flirtatious incident becomes tainted with shame and fear, when it could be something to be enjoyed. Relationships become marked by conflicting feelings. This makes things very difficult when you enter into a close relationship. If you are a straight woman who has been abused by a man, for example, this confusion will most frequently surface when you are attracted to a man now.

Relationships with partners are confusing

One of the core problems of ambivalence for straight women like Eva can be giving off confusing messages to men. Eva is trapped in a cycle of ambivalence. She will find herself attracted to a man and will start to engage him in conversation, or even begin dating him, giving off strong signals that she finds him attractive. Yet suddenly, without warning, she will pull away from him and stop returning his calls, leaving him very shocked. Eva is experiencing ambivalent feelings. She is attracted to men, but as the fear from her past kicks in, she freezes them out, leaving them feeling perplexed and thinking that perhaps they have been the victim of some kind of game.

This can happen on many levels; from a chance meeting with a stranger at a party, to actually being in relationships but running away when a certain level of intimacy is reached. Essentially, sexual ambivalence is confusion. One part wants to engage, but the other part is in touch with the pain of the past and doesn't want to risk that again.

I so identify with this cycle of behaviour! At the beginning of this book I described a break-up with a boyfriend caused mainly by my ambivalent feelings towards men. This pattern carried on for some years with different partners until I met my husband. During the first year of our relationship I finished with him every single Wednesday night! I wanted him but I didn't want him. Finally, he had had enough and was on the point of ending it when I realized that I didn't want to lose him. So I decided to get some professional help. This was a turning point, and through counselling I began to see how fears from my past were manipulating me into running from a situation which deep down I really wanted.

Addiction to sex

This misplaced sexuality can also take another form. Instead of feeling repulsed by sex, some victims of abuse use sex as a way of relieving their pain and gaining a sense of power. Mackenzie was extremely sexually attractive and, like Eva, had no problem getting men's attention. In many ways, being able to attract people in this way raised her self-esteem. Mackenzie had many sexual partners, but took care never to get emotionally involved with them. She did not want to risk being hurt as she had been when she was a child, by an abusive teacher and a family that didn't give her much attention.

However, in the long run Mackenzie's behaviour led to more problems as she began to feel dissatisfied by her various sexual partners. Mackenzie used sex, where there was no risk of intimacy or having to disclose her true self, as a substitute for a proper relationship. Mackenzie also became addicted to the pleasurable feelings of sex. Although these are not in any way bad in themselves, Mackenzie was using sex to run away from her feelings of pain. Escaping into the good feelings of sex did provide temporary relief, but it did not provide her with long-term satisfaction. Her bedroom experiences also began to compound her inner shame and her legitimate desire to have a meaningful relationship.

Friendships can become distorted

Relationships with close friends can also become distorted after you have been sexually abused. This is because the close relationship you had with the abuser as a child was sexualized. Later, as an adult, you can misinterpret your own longings for intimacy as sexuality. This can mean you subconsciously sexualize relationships, either in reality or in fantasy. This leads to incredible problems in relationships. All intimate relationships are at risk of being sexualized as the longing for friendship becomes confused with something else. You may even withdraw from potentially healthy friendships out of fear of crossing a boundary.

• •

Jo-Jo found herself becoming increasingly dependent on her friend Elaine, spending lots of time together and sharing really deep secrets with her. Elaine accepted Jo-Jo's hugs as a deepening of their relationship. Jo-Jo, however, was confused. She knew she was straight, but part of her was becoming increasingly attracted to Elaine. Feeling frightened of this feeling, Jo-Jo quickly broke off the friendship, leaving Elaine very hurt.

Addiction to feeling fearful

If you have ever been on a rollercoaster at a fairground, you will have experienced the thrill and the fear of the ride as you go from dizzy heights to stomach-churning depths. As the adrenaline rushes round your body it can produce an extremely exciting feeling. Although different, if you grew up in a situation where there was a great deal of fear and tension, you will also have experienced a lot of adrenaline rushes. The feelings of panic and adrenaline caused by abuse can become very addictive. This was the case for Mandy. Mandy moved house every few months, even though sometimes she had nowhere to go. She also quit jobs at regular intervals, and most of her relationships were with men who were married. Mandy was addicted to creating crisis. Having lived in crisis for most of her childhood, fearing her mother's violent temper, she needed to create a crisis in order to feel normal. She was used to feeling on the edge, and when her life began to become more stable she found it very unsettling and so would actively destabilize it by moving on.

There are many ways that we can create situations in our own lives to reproduce this feeling of panic. For example, we could take up exciting and fear-inducing activities such as dangerous sports, driving too fast, or indulging in illicit relationships where there is a danger of being "found out". We could also create for ourselves a crisis-filled life, for instance, by frequently moving home when we have nowhere to go. Some of the ways we may do this could be:

- Leaving a job without having another one to go to
- Moving house frequently
- Ending relationships or friendships abruptly
- Putting ourselves in the way of harm
- Having relationships with people who are abusive
- Having relationships with people who are married or not available

How to give up creating crisis

If you find yourself addicted to crisis situations, once again you need to return to the source of the problem: the abuse itself. Of course, we need to realize that excitement is a key part of life – without it we would be really bored. But being addicted to it leads to chaotic living and is ultimately destructive.

Work out how many times you have created a crisis in the last few months, then write down the results. Here are some areas you may want to consider:

Changing jobs

Did that sudden departure from your job lead to a better one or was it just one in a long line of unsatisfactory work choices?

Moving house

Have you constantly changed accommodation in the search for the perfect location or housemates?

Ending relationships

Do you find yourself leaving a friendship or relationship when it starts to get a bit too familiar? Does the excitement of meeting someone new quickly get replaced with boredom so you feel the need to find someone else?

Break the cycle
One way to escape from this cycle is to make yourself stay in a situation longer than you would normally, no matter how bad the job or living conditions are. This will help you to break out of your usual "moving on" timeframe. When Mandy was in her support group, she reached her normal six-month deadline for switching her job. With the support of the group she managed to stay for two months longer. This was a milestone on her journey towards breaking the cycle of creating crisis.

This is a big life change, so you may need support to achieve it. You will also have to get used to forgoing the adrenaline rushes you would normally experience from creating crisis. This means starting to embrace more stable, peaceful feelings. However, it does not mean you have to relinquish all feelings of exhilaration.

Finding other ways to create excitement
There is a fine line between fear and excitement (witness those terrifying rides at fairgrounds). If you crave excitement, try to be creative about ways you can experience it without sabotaging your life. For example, you could consider taking up a sport which is stimulating and stretches you mentally and physically, or going to theme parks that offer "scary" rides.

Overcoming ambivalence in relationships
Overcoming ambivalence is also about keeping your lines of communication open. If you are in a friendship and you are feeling confused or are beginning to sexualize the relationship, acknowledge to yourself that you link intimacy with sex because you have been abused. Try not to make

any rash decisions about your relationships if these sexual feelings creep in. If you think the friendship can take it, try to confide in your friend. Tell them about the problems you are experiencing and how they are linked with your past. If not, then try to seek support elsewhere.

If you are in a sexual relationship, explain to your partner that sexuality and touch are a difficult area for you. This is not about them or their attractiveness. Keep talking and explaining how you are feeling. Try to bring them into your world and help them to understand where you are coming from. Keep them included, rather than on the outside looking in.

Tips for physical relationships

During the years that I have run groups for women who have experienced sexual abuse, the women within the groups have come up with some very practical measures for taking control in relationships when the trauma of sexual confusion starts to kick in. These are a few of the key points the groups have found helpful:

- Build good physical boundaries that you are both happy with. Do this before you start getting physical with each other; often there is not time once things get heated.

- If you are kissing or embracing, keep your eyes open so you stay focused on who you are with and your mind can't be tricked into putting the abuser's face there.

- Ask your partner to keep talking to you, to speak your name, when you are physically intimate – especially if you are having sex. This again will help you to stay in the present.

- If you start having flashbacks during sex, explain to your partner what is happening to you. Work out a plan together that "grounds" you in the here-and-now. You

could try using some of the techniques described in
chapter three.

- Go slowly. Get to know your partner without having
  full-blown sex. Let excitement and trust build. Start with
  hand-holding and gentle kissing.

- Be creative. If you don't want to have sex, find other
  ways to be close to each other, such as sharing a romantic
  dinner together.

- Unite. Become partners in working this problem out
  together.

- If sex is very important to your partner, try not to see
  this as intimidating, but as a picture of what sex could be
  to you, too.

- If your partner does not respect your physical
  boundaries, reconsider the whole relationship. If you
  are in a permanent relationship you may need outside
  support to do this.

Don't go it alone

Being supported and accountable in your relationships is
invaluable. In particular, stay in touch with your support
system when you are dating. Listen to the feedback you
receive from friends and pay attention to the reality checks
they can give you. This is especially important if you are used
to cutting and running. Talking about the difficulties you may
be experiencing helps to put your problems into perspective
and gives you new hope.

If you think you may be entering into frequent sexual
relationships and you are not happy with this, you can get
support from specialized groups such as a twelve-step group
or a counsellor who is experienced in this area.

It is especially important that you don't compromise yourself or your boundaries in the area of your sexuality. Don't allow yourself to suffer more anguish in a part of your life where you have already experienced so much distress. If your date or partner does not listen to you or respect what you feel able to give, then reassess your commitment to them.

If you are in a dating relationship, stop and consider if you really want to stay in the relationship. Do not be afraid of not being with someone who does not respect your sexual choices and requests. If you are in a permanent relationship and your partner continually compromises what you have told them you are happy with, seek professional support as soon as you can.

Checkout sheet: Chapter eight

· ·

1. Have you ever felt fear and longing at the same time?

2. Did this happen when you were in an intimate situation; for example, with a partner?

3. How do you handle being attracted to someone who is attracted to you?

4. Do you think you give off confusing messages to people who find you attractive – for example, flirting with them and then freezing them out?

5. Have you ever felt an attraction to a close friend?

6. Do you think that you subconsciously create crisis because it is exciting?

7. What would you miss if you lived a more balanced and peaceful life?

CHAPTER NINE

FORGIVENESS: HOW WILL THAT HELP ME?

Isabella struggles through Sunday lunch at her family home. Surrounded by her two brothers, mother, and grandfather, she comes every week in order to show that she does not bear a grudge. The family accept that she was abused by her now ailing grandfather, but she has been persuaded to pretend it didn't happen because, in her elder brother's words, "We don't know how long he will be with us." The effort of choking down her dinner in the presence of the man who abused her is causing Isabella untold amounts of distress. However, she comforts herself with the belief that she is acting in forgiveness. But is she?

For many people the idea of forgiving someone who has devastated their life is totally unacceptable – even repulsive. Why forgive someone who has deliberately caused you pain and grief? Isn't that just letting them off the hook? Surely forgiving means you will be losing even more power to your abuser?

Why forgive?
The most important point you need to remember about forgiveness is that you do it for yourself. Archbishop Desmond Tutu, who led the Truth and Reconciliation Commission in South Africa, said: "Holding on to your resentment means you are locked into your victimhood – and you allow your perpetrator to have a hold over your life. When you forgive,

you let go. It sets you free."[1] As I understand it, Reverend Tutu was drawing attention away from the abuser and emphasizing that what is critical about forgiveness is that it will release you from being their victim. Think of yourself and your abuser. If you are constantly consumed by hatred and bitterness towards them, they will be your focus and you will be tied to them still.

What is forgiveness?

First, forgiveness is not denial. You may have heard the expression, "Forgive and forget." This is impossible to do unless you intend to live in denial. We forgive, but the memory still remains. Forgiveness means fully admitting what has happened – allowing yourself to say, "Yes, it was that bad." In order to do this, you need to face up to the harm that has been done to you. Many people think that forgiveness just means overlooking or forgetting what has happened to them. This, however, is another form of denial. Not facing up to the suffering we have gone through is actually a way of avoiding the truth. We have to fully acknowledge the terrible atrocity that has been committed against us; anything less is superficial forgiveness.

Forgiveness is a much more complex process than people think. It takes time and has many layers to it. Forgiveness needs to be extended not only to the people who have harmed us, but also to God (if we have a faith), and even to ourselves.

We often have to forgive several people or groups of people. These may include:

- The abuser
- Other members of our family who may have allowed the abuse to happen
- The community that may also have allowed the abuse to happen

- God, if we have a faith
- Ourselves – for any negative actions we took as a consequence of being abused

Forgiving ourselves

Many of us are buried under layers and layers of guilt which need to be peeled away. We never have to forgive ourselves for the abuse – that was not our choice. However, we do have to forgive ourselves for negative choices we might have made because we were abused. These choices may include:

- Entering into relationships that have damaged us
- Adopting addictive or destructive behaviour patterns
- Not valuing or caring for ourselves
- Harming ourselves

Letting go of the anger we feel towards ourselves for making these choices, without absolving ourselves of personal responsibility, will free us to walk into a new future. Otherwise we could spend the rest of our life filled with regret.

Another way to begin forgiving ourselves is to seek support from friends or a counsellor in dealing with the difficult feelings we may be experiencing.

Who will give me justice?

It is a good point. If we give up our right to revenge, how will we see justice? After all, most societies do not deal well with abusers.

Some communities, however, have found a way to execute their own justice for crimes of this nature. In Canada a community of native Canadians called the Métis carry out their own form of punishment for sexual abuse. This is based on traditional native Canadian concepts of justice founded on the premise that the offender has hurt not only the victim but the whole community. This culminates in a "sentencing circle", where the community decides how the perpetrator should be dealt with. The offender faces a choice: to accept responsibility for their crime and be judged by their victims and community (the circle); or to be handed over to the conventional justice system. If they re-offend after being sentenced by the circle, they are handed over to the police and exiled for ever.[2]

A sentencing circle could, for example, be made up of 200 people from the local community. The inner circle would consist of the victims, a provincial court judge, police officers, and social workers. The rest of the community would sit on the outer circle and watch. These sessions can take up to fourteen hours, during which time everyone involved – from the social workers to the victims – states their case, and how they feel the perpetrator should be treated. The abuser is then sentenced at the end of the session. This usually involves a stay in prison, or probation, and a lengthy and intensive period of counselling.

Unfortunately, in many cultures victims of abuse rarely get to see the justice they deserve. In some faith communities, for example, nothing is said about the abuse and although the abusers may be removed, they subsequently go on to re-offend.

Also, it is a statistical fact that most abuse is contained within families and close communities, and so it often goes unrecognized and unpunished.

Confrontation

It is my experience that confrontation rarely leads to the abuser admitting their guilt. You need to consider this carefully. Confrontation should only be undertaken with extreme caution, and with a lot of outside support both before and afterwards. If you do choose to confront your abuser, you should think carefully about how you will feel afterwards. You also need to think through what the repercussions might be in other areas of your life. You must be clearly aware (especially if you are confronting an abuser who is within your family) that your family could support the abuser and not you. This could then leave you on the outside of the family.

If you are thinking about confronting your abuser, some points you need to consider include:

• What do you hope to gain?
• What could you lose?
• Realistically speaking, what is their response going to be?
• Will the people around you and the abuser support you?
• Can you talk to them first to gauge this?
• Can you take someone else with you?
• Who will be around for you afterwards to support you through the process?

Make sure you line up a close friend or counsellor to talk to directly afterwards if you decide to confront your abuser.

If you are concerned that the abuser still has access to children, contact Social Services or children's protection service. In the UK this is the NSPCC, and they will tell you what steps you should take. Contact details for the NSPCC can be found on page 159.

Forgiveness is a process

Forgiveness is an attitude. It is OK to say, "I forgive as much as I can today." Don't feel under pressure to forgive everything in one go, and don't worry if you can't forgive straight away. At times, you may have to forgive the same things again and again because they are so painful and have caused you so much distress. This does not mean your initial forgiveness was meaningless; rather that you are unpeeling the events one layer at a time. You also need to know that getting in touch with your grief and anger is all part of the process which leads to forgiveness. Deep forgiveness takes time. Give yourself that time.

Here are some questions you may need to ask yourself:

- Do you think this is the right time to consider forgiving?
- Do you need more time first to think through what has happened?
- What would you lose by forgiving?
- What would you gain?

As with the anger exercise on page 71, for some people, thinking about forgiving their abuser is too overwhelming, so don't start with that. Instead, think about someone else who has recently caused you a more minor hurt. Also, you do not have to do this face to face. Why not start by writing it down to make your feelings more tangible. You could consider including:

- What their actions were
- The pain they have caused you
- The subsequent effects on your life and relationships
- How they should have treated you
- What boundaries you are putting up to protect yourself
- Whether you are continuing the relationship or not
- The fact that you are now starting to let go of your anger – at your own pace

If the person admits their guilt and takes responsibility for their actions, you could at that stage consider telling them you have forgiven them – if you are in that place. With support, you could then work towards forgiving other people until you are ready to deal with your abuser.

Forgiveness does not mean being re-abused

Many people do not want to forgive, because they suspect they will just be re-abused. This is a justifiable fear. However, forgiving someone and being reconciled to them is very different. Forgiving does not mean opening yourself up to being abused again. You may forgive, but you may also have to put up strong boundaries to prevent that person from hurting you again.

Forgiveness also does not mean that the abuser can just say "sorry". For any chance of a meaningful reconciliation, the abuser has to show active and genuine signs of change and accountability. These may include:

- Agreeing that the abuse happened
- Accepting responsibility for the abuse
- Showing grief and acknowledging the harm that was done
- Getting counselling or professional help
- Being accountable to a professional body such as a probation officer or social worker [3]

You should not walk back into a trusting relationship with someone who has not acknowledged or changed their abusive behaviour.

Millie was told by her priest that in accordance with her religion, she must go and tell the uncle who molested her as a child that she had forgiven him. Apart from the fact that Millie's priest was using his position as a religious leader in a very manipulative fashion, he was also endangering her. Millie's uncle had not changed. When Millie arrived at his house, unfortunately he was alone and he attempted to assault her. What Millie's priest had omitted to take into account is that there is a big difference between forgiveness and trusting the abuser again. Until there is obvious change, the relationship cannot be truly restored.

• •

Losing time

When you have faced the injustice of abuse, it is totally understandable to want to hang on to resentment and anger. Unfortunately, one of the consequences of this is that we tend to project our anger (often subconsciously) onto other people who remind us of the person who has hurt us. Not only is this unfair on that person, it also puts our relationship with them in jeopardy.

Another consequence of not being able to let go of the past is that you waste your life and time focusing on someone else. Of course it is right to make time to assess the pain and damage you have suffered. However, at some point you need to move on to think about your own life and the choices you want to make, rather than allowing the abuser to steal more precious time from you.

Being open to new relationships

Holding on to the pain means we are hiding behind a wall of self-protection. We can build up these defence systems because help did not come when we needed it. However, in the long term this only leads to a life of loneliness, as we avoid relationships that may cause us pain in the hope of protecting ourselves. In our own minds, we are keeping out anyone who could abuse us further. But this means that we keep out positive and constructive people as well – people who could be really good for us and give us the joy, love, and friendship we deserve.

Forgiveness releases us to live our life, whereas without it we may remain a hostage to someone else's actions. The desire to hold on to feelings of retribution is perfectly understandable, but it is also worth considering that "living well is the best revenge".[4]

Checkout sheet: Chapter nine

. . . .

1. Have you ever hated someone because they reminded you of someone who has hurt you?

2. Do you think you have made negative choices because you were abused?

3. Do you think you are still holding these things against yourself?

4. Have you thought of confronting your abuser?

5. Is there anyone who could support you through this process?

6. What might you lose by thinking about the process of forgiving?

7. What might you gain?

8. Is there anyone you could express your fears about forgiving to?

CHAPTER TEN

A NEW BEGINNING: DREAMS CAN COME TRUE

"Life is not so much a matter of 'finding' ourselves as it is a process of making ourselves."[1] This is a very empowering statement. We may not have had the ideal childhood, or the basic foundations that would have made our early adult life easy, but that does not mean the rest of our life has to be shaped by our past.

Through our own efforts and the support of others, we can rebuild and restore our lives and defy the legacy of our childhood. Perhaps even by reading this book you feel you are further on than when you started. This is good news! Our lives are changed step by step as we face each issue, taking one day at a time.

Dreaming new dreams

Have you ever let your mind run free and allowed yourself the luxury of dreaming wild dreams about your future? Not empty fantasies based on our celebrity culture, but a career you would really like to follow, a qualification you would like to have, or perhaps a book you would like to write.

Write down some of the projects and ideas you would love to pursue if time and money were no limit! Are they really that unattainable? Is lack of education stopping you from moving ahead? Is it possible to catch up by doing home study or evening courses?

What about on an emotional level? Would you like to be in better relationships, or even to enter a relationship? Perhaps you need a little help and guidance in these areas. If you have not done so already, consider investing in some counselling or joining a support group.

Relationships

When we choose to relate to another person and even to love them, we choose to face the possibility of gaining great happiness as well as risking great pain. Although this may be the last thing we feel like doing, the only way to break out of isolation is to go ahead and take that risk. We need to bear in mind, however, as discussed in chapter six, that there are boundaries we can put in place to help us to have healthy relationships and not destructive ones.

It would be worth looking, for example, at how we could expand our circle of friends.

When problems come

Everyone has problems! But there are ways to deal with problems so that they don't overwhelm us. Here is a simple plan of action to help you to face problems when they arise:

Acknowledge the problem

By owning the problem you gain distance from it. Then there is hope for change.

Take an inventory

Write down how much or little the problem affects and controls you.

Seek counsel

Find someone you trust and ask their advice.

Accountability

Problems worsen when you try to deal with your situation alone, so make sure there is support around you. Here is an example of what steps you could take if you found, for instance, that you were drinking more than you used to.

- First, acknowledge that you are drinking more and that it is causing you concern
- Next, write down when you are likely to drink – is this at times of stress, or loneliness?
- Thirdly, think through how it is affecting your life. Perhaps you are finding it hard to get up in the morning, or you are looking unhealthy, etc.
- Find a friend who knows you quite well and talk to them about it
- If there isn't anyone you could talk to, or you feel you would like input from a professional, consider getting in touch with a counsellor or an organization that could give you support – for example, Alcoholics Anonymous
- Finally, stay in touch with your support systems even after the initial problem has gone away. That's hard, but it's the key way to find a long-term resolution to your difficulty

"Accountability" isn't a popular word today. People like to do their own thing and don't want other people knowing too much about them. And yet the very reason that abuse continues to happen is that individuals and families are simply not accountable to anyone. There is nothing more destructive for society than people becoming isolated, hidden away behind closed doors with no one knowing if they need help. Being accountable to someone simply means that you keep in touch with them and that they are there for you at times when you need a little extra support.

This is the whole basis on which groups such as Alcoholics Anonymous run. The group supports those within it and makes it easier for them to live lives which are free from the negative effects of drugs and alcohol. Try to think of someone you could trust to help you with the issues you are dealing with. It could be a friend, or a social worker or counsellor if you have one. You could also consider joining a support group: you can find out about these through your doctor or Social Services. There are also co-dependency groups based on the Alcoholics Anonymous principles that you can join. There is a list of organizations that can help you at the back of this book.

New self-perceptions [2]

Many of us have very bad internal PR! We need to develop new internal messages and perceptions. This is a long process, but we can begin by identifying what we think about ourselves through listing some of our recurring thought patterns.

Take a look at how you see yourself in different areas of your life. How do you feel about:

• Yourself?

• How you behave in relationships?

• How you behave at work?

• How you look?

Write down the first words or phrases that come to mind, no matter how bad they might be! These could include:

• Sad

• Bored

• Ugly

• Withdrawn

• Frustrated

- Angry
- Unhappy

Then write down a similar list of positive qualities. If you
need help with this, why not ask your friends or, if you have
one, your counsellor. You may want to include words like:

- Talented
- Pretty
- Engaging
- Kind

It is these positive perceptions that you need to focus on and
try to substitute for your old negative thinking patterns. Your
old perceptions will not automatically go away, but you can
limit them with your new thoughts and ideas. Whereas your
old patterns of thinking are already well established, you will
need to reinforce your new perceptions by bringing them to
mind regularly. To do this, you may need to practise saying
them, or even write them down on a card or your phone and
look at them frequently.

We are all on a journey and most of us will have issues of
some kind that we need to deal with. But we can get to a place
where we judge ourselves less harshly and find more creative
solutions to our problems instead.

Helping others
Perhaps the most critical questions asked by people who
have suffered abuse are, "Can I ever get over this?" and
"Can anyone really understand what I have been through?"
From a personal point of view, I can say that reaching out to
others who have also been through the experience of sexual
abuse has really empowered me. Somehow for me it has
made the journey more worthwhile, and I am so thankful

to have met so many brave and inspiring men and women along the way.

I'm not sure whether I can say that I am glad the abuse happened to me, but contrary to my earlier beliefs, it hasn't finished me off! It has made me a different kind of person from the one I would have been had I not been abused, but maybe that is not a bad thing. I think it has made me more sensitive to others and has given me an ability to see the pain in the lives of those around me, whether or not they have experienced abuse. This in turn has enabled me to get closer to them and to reach out to them more effectively.

It's a rollercoaster ride!

Recovering from sexual abuse is a bit like getting onto a fairground ride. You go up and down. When you first start to look back at your life and the damage that you have suffered, your emotions can often take a dip as you relive the pain a second time. However, as you start to examine your past and work through the feelings this brings up, your emotions begin to go through a period of transition. At the end of this process you will end up feeling stronger and better than when you started. You may go through several highs and lows as you continue, but the good periods begin to last longer and the lows are not as low. Change becomes more sustained and permanent. Additionally, when life does throw things at you, you will find you are more able to navigate your journey.

The time is now

Finally, I was in a meeting at my church some time ago, and suddenly the speaker, Dr Yinka Adewole, turned to us and said, "When is the most important time in your life?" Various suggestions were made: "When I got married", "When my daughter was born", or "When I passed my degree".

But Dr Yinka stopped everyone and said, "No, this is all wrong. Now is the most important time because now is the only time."

This is so true. Now is the only time. We can learn to take life one day at a time – to take each decision step by step, living in the moment as much as we can.

I was feeling afraid that day of certain people in my life, and my insecurities began to come flooding back. I asked Dr Yinka for help. He took me aside and said to me, "You aren't here to be afraid of anyone – you are here to love people. Now that puts you in control."

He was right. Our lives may be partially shaped by our past, but we don't have to let it define us. We may have been disempowered and manipulated, but we can (healthily!) take control of our lives now.

Let's not miss out on the power that is ours – the power to live, and to love, and to realize our dreams.

Checkout sheet: Chapter ten

• •

1. Do you think you have gained any useful information or help from this book?

2. Which chapter have you most identified with?

3. Do you feel you have gained any insight into your behaviour?

4. Do you have any crazy dreams for the future?

5. What stops you from fulfilling those dreams? Are they real obstacles or imagined ones?

6. Write down your wildest dream.

7. Congratulate yourself – you have finished the book. Well done!

ENDNOTES

Chapter One

1. L. Kelly, L. Regan, and S. Burton, "Prevalence of Sexual Abuse", Child and Women Abuse Studies Unit of North London, 1991. This was a survey of 1,244 young people attending further education colleges in Britain.
2. Diana Russell, *The Secret Trauma*, Basic Books, 1986.
3. David Finkelhor et al., "Sexual Abuse in a national survey of adult men and women: prevalence characteristics and risk factors", Child Abuse and Neglect, 1990.
4. Pat Cawson et al., "Child maltreatment in the UK: a study of the prevalence of child abuse and neglect", NSPCC, 2000.
5. www.nspcc.org.uk/inform/publications
6. http://www.bbc.co.uk/asia pacific/social customs and sexual abuse
7. www.childline.org.uk
8. NSPCC factsheet, April 2010.
9. Diana Russell, *The Secret Trauma*, Basic Books, 1986.
10. Lisa Bunting, "Females who sexually offend against children: responses of the child protection and criminal justice systems", NSPCC, 2005.
11. www.nspcc.org.uk
12. Dr Nicola Madge, *Abuse and Survival: A Fact File*, The Princes Trust, 1997.
13. HM Inspectorate of Prisons, *Women in Prison: A thematic review*. Home Office, 1997.
14. R. Acierno, *Behavioural Medicine* 23(2) 1997, pp. 53–64.
15. V. Fellitti and R. Anda, "Adverse childhood experiences", *American Journal of Preventative Medicine* 14, 1998, pp. 245–58.
16. S. Porter, "Assault experiences among drug users", *Substance Misuse Bulletin* 8(1), 1994.

Chapter Two

1. Penny Parks, *Rescuing the Inner Child*, Human Horizons Series, 1990, p. 43.
2. Based loosely on an idea in Heiritter, L., and Vought, J., *Helping Victims of Sexual Abuse*, Bethany House Publishers, 1989, p. 154.

Chapter Three

1. John Briere and Jon Conte, "Self-Reported Amnesia for Abuse in Adults Molested as Children", *Journal of Traumatic Stress*, Vol. 6. No. I, 1993.
2. www.oxforddictionaries.com
3. A common exercise on many rape crisis websites including the Worcester Rape Crisis Centre website: http://www.wrsasc.org.uk/advice7.html

Chapter Four
1. Neil Clark Warren, *Make Anger Your Ally*, Tyndale House, 1990, p. 113.
2. Emily Bronte, *Wuthering Heights*, Penguin Popular Classics, 1995 edn.
3. Julie Bindel, "I took all my anger out on him", *The Guardian*, 16/8/2005.

Chapter Five
1. Ralph Waldo Emerson, source unknown.
2. Hemfelt, Minirth, and Meier, *Love is a Choice*, Monarch Publications, 1990, p. 64.
3. These family roles are based loosley on an idea in Hemfelt, Minirth, and Meier, *Love is a Choice*, Monarch Publications, 1990, pp. 157–58. These roles were first described in Wegscheider-Cruse, Sharon, *Another Chance: Hope and Health for the Alcoholic Family*, Science and Behavior Books.

Chapter Six
1. www.childline.org.uk
2. Based on ideas in Cloud and Townsend, *Boundaries*, Zondervan Press, 1992, p. 59.
3. Based on an idea in Allender, Dan B., *The Wounded Heart: Hope for Adult Victims of Childhood Sexual Abuse*, NavPress; 1990., p. 115.
4. Based on an idea in Allender, *The Wounded Heart*, p. 118.
5. Based on an idea in Cloud, H., and Townsend, J., *Boundaries in Dating: Making Dating Work*, Zondervan; 2000, p. 230.

Chapter Seven
1. Hemfelt, Minirth, and Meier, *Love is a Choice*, Monarch Publications, 1990, p. 64.
2. Based loosley on an idea in Hemfelt, Minirth, and Meier, *Love is a Choice*, Monarch Publications, 1990, p. 184.

Chapter Eight
1. John Gray, *Mars and Venus in the Bedroom*, Vermillion, 1997, p. 13.

Chapter Nine
1. BBC News website: www.bbc.co.uk: 27/2/2006
2. Based on an idea in Allender, Dan B., *The Wounded Heart: Hope for Adult Victims of Childhood Sexual Abuse*, NavPress; 1990., p. 236.
3. Julie Wainwright, "Generations of Sexual Abuse How One Town is Breaking The Cycle", *Marie Clare*, November 1998.
4. George Herbert, "Jacula Prudentum", *The Complete Works in verse and prose of George Herbert*, Volume III, Prose (1874), ed Rev. Alexander B. Grosart.

Chapter Ten
1. Alan Loy McGinnis, *Confidence*, Marshall Pickering,1987, p. 43.
2. Based loosley on an idea in Hemfelt, Minirth, and Meier, *Love is a Choice*, Monarch Publications, 1990, p. 244.

FINDING FURTHER SUPPORT IN THE UK

Adult Male Survivors of Sexual Abuse
Helpline, counselling, group work, information, and resources for men who have been abused or raped. Based in Swindon.
Tel: 0845 430 9371   Website: www.amsosa.com

Alcoholics Anonymous
Provides help and support around alcohol issues.
Website: www.alcoholics-anonymous.org

Association of Christian Counsellors
Can recommend a counsellor in your area who holds Christian beliefs.
Website: www.acc-uk.org

Beating Eating Disorders
Information and help on all aspects of eating disorders, including anorexia nervosa, bulimia nervosa, binge eating, and related eating disorders.
Website: www.b-eat.co.uk

Breaking Free – Female Support Project
Email and helpline support. Also counselling based in Swindon.
Tel: 07547 680839   Website: www.breakingfreesupport.co.uk

British Association for Counselling and Psychotherapy
Professional counselling body which can recommend a counsellor in your area.
Tel: 0870 443 5252   Website: www.bacp.co.uk

ChildLine
Offers help and counsel to children.
Tel: 0800 1111   Website: www.childline.org.uk

Churches Child Protection Advisory Service
Professional body specializing in child protection support and training.
Website: www.ccpas.co.uk

Directory and Book Service Pathfinder
Free support and information for survivors of child abuse, incest, and rape.
Tel: 01255 675351   Website: www.dabspathfinder.org

Into the Light
Provides information, training, and resources in the area of sexual abuse.
Website: www.intothelight.org.uk

Life Centre
Confidential counselling services for male and female survivors of all types of sexual abuse, past and present.
Tel: 01243 786349   Website: www.lifecentre.uk.com

Mosac
Supports non-abusive parents and carers whose children have been sexually abused.
Website: www.mosac.org.uk

Narcotics Anonymous
Provides help and support around drug issues.
Website: www.na.org

National Association for People Abused in Childhood
Information and resources for people who have experienced all kinds of child abuse.
Tel: 0800 0853330   Website: www.napac.org.uk

NSPCC
Twenty-four-hour child protection helpline.
Tel: 0808 8005000   Website: www.nspcc.org.uk

One in Four
A registered charity which provides support and resources to people who have experienced sexual abuse and sexual violence. Run for and by people who have experienced sexual abuse.
Tel: 0208 697 2112   Website: www.oneinfour.org.uk

Overeaters Anonymous
Provides help and support around eating disorders.
Website: www.oagb.org.uk

Penny Parks Foundation
Provides effective, fast, and painless therapy and training for the resolution of child abuse trauma.
Website: www.ppfoundation.org

Rape and Abuse Line
Offers free, confidential support to anyone affected by rape and/or abuse issues for both female and male survivors.
Website: www.rapeandabuseline.co.uk

Rape and Sexual Abuse Support Centre
Supports women survivors of rape and sexual abuse through face-to-face counselling and a helpline.
Tel: 0808 802 9999   Website: www.rasasc.org.uk

Rape Crisis
Specialist services for women and girls who have been raped in England and Wales.
Website: www.rapecrisis.org.uk

Samaritans
Provide a twenty-four-hour listening service as well as emotional support online.
Website: www.samaritans.co.uk

Step Up
A support service for families where children have been sexually abused or raped.
Website: www.step-up-charity.co.uk

Stop It Now
A public education campaign aimed at preventing child sexual abuse by increasing public awareness.
Website: www.stopitnow.org.uk

Survivors Network
Provides email and helpline support and counsel to women survivors of rape and sexual abuse.
Tel: 01273 720110   Website: www.survivorsnetwork.org.uk

Survivors Trust
A national umbrella agency supporting specialist services for survivors of rape and sexual abuse.

Website: www.thesurvivorstrust.org

Survivors UK
Provides help and counselling for male survivors of rape and sexual abuse.
Tel: 0845 1221201   Website: www.survivorsuk.org

Trauma and Abuse Group (TAG)
A group studying and supporting work concerning trauma, abuse, and dissociation.
Website: www.tag-uk.net

Trauma and Abuse Support Centre (TASC)
A resource for survivors of child sexual abuse providing links to other organizations, articles, news, events, and a book store.
Website: www.tasc-online.org.uk

United Kingdom Council for Psychotherapy
Professional body for psychotherapists, which can recommend a psychotherapist in your area.
Website: www.psychotherapy.org.uk

Victim Support
Helps people cope with the after effects of crime, offering support and information.
Website: www.victimsupport.org.uk

Women and Girls Network
National helpline offering support and advice to women who have experienced child sexual abuse, rape, and domestic violence.
Tel: 0207 510 4345   Website: www.wgn.org.uk